The Scottish Beer Bible

A selection of beer labels from defunct Scottish breweries

THE SCOTTISH

MERCAT PRESS

THE ESSENTIAL GUIDE
TO OVER 150 SCOTTISH
BEERS AND LAGERS

EDINBURGH

BEER BIBLE

Gavin D. Smith

Beauty lies in the hands of the beerholder
—W. C. Fields

MERCAT PRESS
EDINBURGH
www.mercatpress.com

First published in 2001 by Mercat Press
James Thin, 53 South Bridge, Edinburgh EH1 1YS
www.mercatpress.com

ISBN 184183 0216

*For the beer-makers and beer-drinkers of Scotland,
past and present*

Set in Caslon at Mercat Press
Printed and bound in Spain by Santamaria

Contents

List of Illustrations

Acknowledgements

My thanks go to the following for their time, interest, enthusiasm and shared knowledge: Chris Anderson, Colin Blackwood, Mark Briggs, Nick Bromfield, Ken and Ingrid Brooker, Rob Bruce, Ian Cameron, Fergus and Ailish Clark, Seán Costello, Jack Cumming, Ron Davies, Samantha Faircliff, Brian Flynn, Richard Gibb, John Gibson, David Gladwin, Robin Graham, Ian Hallam, Jim Henderson, George Howell, Tom Johnstone, David Jones, Richard Jones, Carl Justice, Duncan Kellock, John McDougall, Angus MacRuary, Peter Martin, Catherine Maxwell Stuart, Alistair Mouat, Fiona Murdoch, Lynn Pretswell, Sonny Priest, Helen Riach, Richard Roberts, Scott Robertson, Douglas Ross, Russell Sharp, Nick Silk, Kerry Teakle, Chris Tomlinson, Alma Topen of the Scottish Brewing Archive, Iain Turnbull, Caroline Wengel, Roger White, Bruce Williams, Colin Youngson, and the staff of the A. K. Bell Library in Perth, the Central Library in Dundee, Clackmannanshire Libraries, the Mitchell Library in Glasgow, and the National Library of Scotland.

The illustrations on pages 11, 16, 19, 20, 26, 27, 28 and 31 are reproduced by kind permission of the Scottish Brewing Archive, while that on page 18 is courtesy of James Simpson.

Anyone who writes about the history of Scottish brewing owes a particular debt of gratitude to Charles McMaster, whose work has done much to stimulate interest in, and increase knowledge of, the subject.

Biographical Note

Gavin D. Smith is a journalist, author and broadcaster. He specialises in horse racing and whisky and writes on both subjects for a wide range of newspapers and magazines. He is the author of six whisky-related books. As a broadcaster he has contributed to a number of BBC Radio Scotland programmes, including *The Right Track*, a series about the Scottish horse-racing scene.

Among his publications are *An A-Z of Whisky* (1997), *Gavin D. Smith's Lake District* (1997) and *A Century of Scotch Whisky* (2001).

He lives in Perth.

Introduction

Mention 'Scotland' and 'drink' in the same sentence, and almost everyone thinks of whisky. The country is rightly proud of its native dram and the important contribution that it makes to the British economy. Scotch whisky also acts as a wonderful ambassador for its homeland all around the world. Yet brewing in Scotland almost certainly predates distilling by many centuries, and has arguably played a greater part in the economic and social life of the nation.

The difference, however, is that whisky has been so shrewdly marketed that it has come to be regarded as an essential element of 'Scottishness', in the same way as tartan or the poetry of Robert Burns. There is a perceived mystique about Scotch whisky and about the manner in which it is made. Certainly, whisk(e)y is distilled in other parts of the world, but for many people, whisky *is* Scotch. Scottish beer, on the other hand, is just beer. There is a common perception that a bottle of beer brewed in Edinburgh is not radically different from one that has its origins in Milwaukee, and that perception is as prevalent in Scotland as it is anywhere else.

During recent years, however, the Scottish brewing industry has undergone a mini-renaissance, and there has been a welcome increase in the number of working breweries. The latest opened in Stornoway on the Isle of Lewis in the spring of 2001. With that increase has come geographical and stylistic diversity. Breweries of vastly differing sizes, and with vastly differing degrees of financial stability, presently operate from the Borders to Shetland's northernmost isle. Products range from traditional cask heavies and pale ales through Czech-style lagers to ale brewed using seaweed.

The profile of Scottish beers has been raised by their growing visibility in bottled format on the shelves of the major supermarkets, off-licence chains, and in specialist outlets and restaurants, but there is a long way to go until the output of Scotland's best breweries enjoys the same cachet as single malt whiskies. Maybe that day will never dawn, but this seems a good time to celebrate and chronicle the vibrant Scottish brewing scene that exists at the beginning of the third millennium.

There is an old saying that it is difficult to appreciate where we are and where we are going if we don't know where we have been. Accordingly, as well as providing a working guide to the present-day Scottish brewing industry in the pages that follow, there is an examination of the long and proud heritage that lies behind, and inevitably influences, current activities.

Ideally, this book should be accompanied by a glass or two of something brewed in Scotland, and, best of all, by something the reader is tasting for the first time. Enjoy—and keep tasting.

BREWING BEER AND LAGER: THE BASICS

The basic ingredients for making beer are malted barley, hops and water, though sugar and finings also play their part, and some brewers produce beers using amounts of unmalted, roasted barley, wheat flour or maize.

During malting, the barley is soaked with water before being heated in order to induce germination. This releases the natural sugars that are essential if fermentation is to occur later in the brewing process. Once the grains of barley begin to produce rootlets, they are roasted in order to prevent too great a degree of germination taking place.

Brewers differentiate between 'pale' and 'dark' malts, and the degree of malting is controlled by varying the temperature. High temperatures make for dark malt, which will produce darker-coloured beer with a 'roasted' flavour. Paler malts, created at lower temperatures, will give beer a lighter colour and a more delicate

Malting floor at James Aitken & Co's Falkirk Brewery, 1880s

and sweet character. Brewers may use just one type of malt to produce a beer, or they may mix several styles to achieve the particular effect they are seeking.

Once malted, the barley is ground in a mill to release soluble starch, and becomes known as 'grist'. This is mixed with pure hot water—rather confusingly called 'liquor'—in the mash tun to produce a 'mash'. The process of mashing converts the soluble starches released by milling into fermentable and non-fermentable sugars, and the resultant liquid is called 'wort'.

The wort is subsequently boiled in a copper, where hops are added, in order to give the beer bitterness, act as a preservative, and kill any bacteria that may be present. The brewer will often add a number of different varieties of hop in order to achieve precisely the flavour he desires in his finished beer.

After a period of up to two hours in the copper, the wort is run through a hop-back, where the used hops are removed, and the liquid then flows into a fermenting vessel, via a heat exchanger which reduces its temperature.

The brewery's own distinctive strain of yeast is added to the wort in the fermenting vessel, and alcohol and carbon dioxide are the result of the yeast's interaction with the fermentable sugars during a period of around five days.

If the beer is to be kegged, bottled or canned, it is chilled, filtered and pasteurised at this point, to ensure that no secondary fermentation occurs. Secondary fermentation is, however, a feature of 'bottle-conditioned' beers.

Coppers at McEwan's Brewery, Edinburgh, 1957

Staff at the Holyrood Brewery, Edinburgh, skimming yeast off fermenting vessel, c.1960

If it is to be sold as 'cask ale', the beer is transferred from the fermenting vessel into conditioning tanks, where it matures for a period of several days, before being 'racked' into casks. During conditioning, finings are added to make the residual yeast settle to the bottom of the vessel, giving a clear beer, and 'priming sugar' is introduced in order to encourage secondary fermentation in the cask. In some cases, dry hops are added during racking, along with additional priming sugar.

Fermentation continues in the cask, which is 'tapped' a couple of days before the beer is due to be served, allowing natural gas to escape via porous venting pegs in the bung-hole.

In lager production, 'bottom-fermenting yeasts' are used, rather than the traditional top-fermenters. These yeasts ferment at much lower temperatures than top-fermenting varieties, and the process takes up to four weeks in cold storage conditions. The name 'lager' is derived from the German verb 'to store'. Lager uses lightly-kilned malts, and is usually lighter in colour and more 'transparent' than most ales.

SCOTTISH BEER TERMINOLOGY

Roger Protz (*The Real Ale Drinker's Almanac*) notes: 'Traditional Scottish beer is quite different in character from English ale. Roasted barley or dark and chocolate malt give a darker and nut-sweet character to beer, and the lack of a hop industry means that hops are used more sparingly.'

Peculiar to Scotland is the use of the term 'shilling' to denote different types and strengths of beer. This system was introduced in 1880, when Beer Duty was first imposed. The shillings were the 'list' price per barrel, but really only served as an indicator of the strength and type of beer, rather an actual indication of how much had been paid for it. The weakest beers would be '28 shillings', ranging up through 'Light' at 42, 'Mild' at 48, Pale Ale at 54 to 60 shillings, 'Export' at 70 and 80 shillings, and Strong ales at up to 15 guineas (315 shillings!).

Protz writes that in Scotland 'low-gravity ale is called "light", even when it is dark or walnut brown in colour, medium ale is "heavy", while stronger "export" ale recalls the great, pioneering days of Scottish brewing when the likes of Younger refreshed the American, Indian and Australian colonies.'

With the development of keg ales, a new term entered the lexicon of Scottish brewing, namely 'Special', which is essentially a carbonated equivalent to Heavy.

MEASUREMENT OF BEER STRENGTH

The strength of beer is indicated either by reference to its 'original gravity' or by measuring its 'alcohol by volume'. The latter denotes the amount of alcohol present in the beer, and is expressed as a percentage. The stronger the beer, the higher the percentage. Alcohol by volume figures are used throughout this book.

CAMRA AND SCOTTISH BEER FESTIVALS

Up-to-date details of the numerous Scottish beer festivals that are staged under the auspices of CAMRA each year are available from The Campaign for Real Ale Ltd, 230 Hatfield Road, St Albans, Hertfordshire AL1 4LW. Tel. 01727 867201/Fax. 01727 867670. Email: camra@camra.org.uk; website: www.camra.org.uk

CAMRA has nine Scottish branches, representing the whole country. The organisation's Scottish Director can be contacted by email at: R.D.Scotland&NI@camra.org.uk

Heritage

IN THE BEGINNING

The early development of brewing is thought to have centred on Mesopotamia between 8,000 and 6,000BC, spreading through Greece, Egypt and eventually to the heart of the Roman Empire. Some commentators claim that brewing was introduced to Britain by the Romans in 55AD, but it was almost certainly widespread in the British Isles by the time of the Roman invasion.

We are led to believe that the Romans preferred the grape to the grain, with the Emperor Julian writing of British beer 'Who made you and from what, by the true Bacchus, I know not. He smells of nectar, but you smell of goat.'

In pre-Roman times, beer—of a sort—was brewed in Scotland from the coarse grain known as bigg, and from corn-weed or darnel, along with natural additives designed to make it more palatable. Brewing can be traced to the Isle of Rum around 3,000BC, and it has been claimed that the Picts were making heather ale by 325BC, though the first documented reference to 'the Picts' only occurs during the third century AD.

A Manchester archaeological researcher, Merryn Dineley, has suggested that brewing may have been taking place on Orkney in Neolithic times, around 3100BC, citing as evidence the discovery of a 30-gallon, bucket-shaped ceramic pot found at Skara Brae.

Heather, meadowsweet and royal fern were used to make beer on Rum, according to botanists from Edinburgh's Royal Botanic Gardens, who spent two years during the 1990s researching the uses of native Scottish plants. Indeed, as Bruce Williams of Heather Ale Ltd has pointed out, a very wide range of botanical ingredients must have been incorporated into Scottish ales at various times, and in addition to his Fraoch heather ale, Williams has created ales using pine (first introduced by the Vikings), elderberry (probably used in brewing from the ninth century) and gooseberries (incorporated into Scottish ale from at least the sixteenth century).

According to F. Marian McNeill in *The Scots Cellar*, 'When the navigator Pytheas visited the land that was to become Scotland, he found that the Picts were skilled in brewing a potent drink, and it has been suggested that the Scots were lured from Eire to Alba by the fame of its heather ale, as the Romans are alleged to have been lured to Britain by the fame of its oyster-beds.'

Historians insist that there is no proven link between the Picts and the production of heather ale, but that did not prevent Robert Louis Stevenson from penning a poem on the subject:

HEATHER ALE
A Galloway Romance
by Robert Louis Stevenson

From the bonny bells of heather
    They brewed a drink long-syne,
Was sweeter far than honey,
    Was stronger far than wine.
They brewed it and they drank it,
    And lay in a blessed swound
For days and days together
    In their dwellings underground.

There rose a king in Scotland,
    A fell man to his foes,
He smote the Picts in battle,
    He hunted them like roes.
Over miles of the red mountain
    He hunted as they fled,
And strewed the dwarfish bodies
    Of the dying and the dead.

Summer came in the country,
    Red was the heather bell;
But the manner of the brewing
    Was none alive to tell.
In graves that were like children's
    On many a mountain head,
The Brewsters of the Heather
    Lay numbered with the dead.

The king in the red moorland
    Rode on a summer's day;
And the bees hummed, and the curlews
    Cried beside the way.
The king rode, and was angry,
    Black was his brow and pale,
To rule in a land of heather
    And lack the Heather Ale.

It fortuned that his vassals,
    Riding free on the heath,
Came on a stone that was fallen
    And vermin hid beneath.
Rudely plucked from their hiding,
    Never a word they spoke:
A son and his aged father—
    Last of the dwarfish folk.

The king sat high on his charger,
    He looked on the little men;
And the dwarfish and swarthy couple
    Looked at the king again.

Down by the shore he had them;
    And there on the giddy brink—
'I will give you life, ye vermin,
    For the secret of the drink.'

There stood the son and father
    And they looked high and low;
The heather was red around them,
    The sea rumbled below.
And up and spoke the father,
    Shrill was his voice to hear:
'I have a word in private,
    A word for the royal ear.

'Life is dear to the aged,
    And honour a little thing;
I would gladly sell the secret,'
    Quoth the Pict to the King.
His voice was small as a sparrow's,
    And shrill and wonderful clear:
'I would gladly sell my secret,
    Only my son I fear.

'For life is a little matter,
    And death is nought to the young;
And I dare not sell my honour
    Under the eye of my son.
Take him, O king, and bind him,
    And cast him far in the deep;
And it's I will tell the secret
    That I have sworn to keep.'

They took the son and bound him,
    Neck and heels in a thong,
And a lad took him and swung him,
    And flung him far and strong,
And the sea swallowed his body,
    Like that of a child of ten;—
And there on the cliff stood the father,
    Last of the dwarfish men.

'True was the word I told you:
    Only my son I feared;
For I doubt the sapling courage
    That goes without the beard.
But now in vain is the torture,
    Fire shall never avail:
Here dies in my bosom
    The secret of Heather Ale.'

The brewing of heather ale largely died out after the Act of Union in 1707, when brewers were required by law to make ale using only malt, hops, yeast and water. The art of brewing heather ale survived in parts of the Highlands and Western Isles, however. Indeed, it was still being produced on Islay when Thomas Pennant visited in 1774. He wrote that ale was made on the island using 'the tops of young heath, mixed with a third part of malt and a few hops'.

The new, post-union legislation stipulating which ingredients could be used in brewing was enacted partly to ensure that narcotic substances were not inadvertently—or deliberately—introduced, though cynics also point out that it created additional income for hop farmers, many of whom happened to be members of the House of Lords!

Traditionally, there was a material difference between 'ale' and 'beer', which has long since been eroded. Originally, 'ale' was brewed without the use of hops, while 'beer' was a continental interloper, finding its way to Britain during the fifteenth century. The hops in beer—first used in at least the late Anglo-Saxon period, and perhaps even before the eighth century—helped to keep it in good condition, while the strength and sweetness of ale had much the same preservative effects. Over time, the rivalry between the two brewing camps disappeared, and hops gained almost universal acceptance. In Scotland, however, fewer hops were used than in England, principally because of the difficulty of cultivating them north of the border.

McNeill writes that 'The term beer was originally used to describe beer brewed with an infusion of hops, but in the trade, *beer* is now the generic name for all malted liquors, *ale* being commonly, though by no means exclusively, used for those of lighter colour'.

Alfred Barnard makes the claim in his *The Noted Breweries of Great Britain & Ireland* (1889-91) that 'Although malt liquor of some kind was used in Egypt in 450BC it was not until 1482 that beer, as we know it, was introduced into Scotland, having, a tradition says, been brewed first by the monks of Banff, and then at Blackford for King James. Beer was not brewed in England until ten years later, its birth being jointly appropriated by Newcastle-on-Tyne and Stone, in Staffordshire.' Presumably, for Barnard, 'beer as we know it' was made with hops.

After his coronation at Scone, near Perth, in 1488, King James IV purchased a barrel of ale from Blackford in Perthshire for twelve shillings (Scots), and it is also thought that the brewery made an 'occasional' ale for the coronation. In 1503 the monarch issued a Royal Charter, officially sanctioning the brewing of ale at Blackford.

Barnard makes the point that it was monks who were the brewers at Banff, and for several centuries brewing in Scotland remained largely the preserve of ecclesiastical bodies. As long ago as the twelfth century, monks sank a well at the base of Arthur's Seat, thus beginning what was to become one of Edinburgh's most significant industries, and records show that in 1219 King Alexander II employed a brewer by the name of Nicholas.

Along with Holyrood, monks brewed at Dunbar (see **Belhaven**) and Newbattle, a few miles south-east of the capital. Arbroath Abbey was another significant centre for ecclesiastical brewing, and McNeill notes that the abbey 'consumed in the thirteenth century more chalders of malt than of all other grains, untreated, put together'.

EXPANSION AND DEVELOPMENT

It was only in the fifteenth century that brewing broke out of its monastic confines, and domestic and commercial breweries began to develop. According to McNeill, in 1495 'the abbot and monks of Cupar [in Fife] granted the right of brewing to certain tenants'. In 1596 a Society of Brewers was formed in Edinburgh, which suggests that commercial brewing was well established on a comparatively large scale by then. Until the eighteenth century, however, most brewing was undertaken either for domestic consumption or on licensed premises. The brewing historian and writer Charles McMaster has pointed out that in 1700 there were 522 'brewers' in the county of Fife alone!

Until the eighteenth century, brewing was predominantly undertaken by women, and a record of Aberdeen brewers for 1509 lists 153 names, only one of which is male. The Edinburgh poet Allan Ramsay (1684-1758) penned a number of poems that give an insight into early eighteenth-century Scottish brewing and tavern life, most notably, perhaps, his 1713 *Elegy on Maggy Johnstoun*:

> AULD REEKY, MOURN IN SABLE HUE!
> *Let fouth of tears dreep like May-dew!*
> *To braw tippony bid adieu,*
> *Which we with greed*
> *Bended as fast as she could brew:—*
> *But ah! She's dead.*
> *Ae summer nights I was sae fou,*
> *Amang the riggs I gaed to spew;*
> *Syne down on a green bawk, I trow*
> *I took a nap,*
> *And soucht a night balillilow,*
> *As sound's a tap.*
> *And when the dawn begoud to glow,*
> *I hirsled up my dizzy pow,*
> *Frae 'mang the corn like wirrycow,*
> *Wi' bains sae sair,*
> *And ken'd nae mair than if a yow*

> *How I came there.*
> *Some said it was the pith of broom*
> *That she stow'd in her masking-loom,*
> *Which in our heads rais'd sic a stoom;*
> *Or some wild seed,*
> *Which aft the chaping stoup did toom,*
> *But fill'd our head.*
> *Then farewell, Maggy, douce and fell,*
> *Of brewers a' thou beur the bell;*
> *[at] a' thy gossies yelp and yell,*
> *And without feed,*
> *Guess whether ye're in heaven or hell,*
> *They're sure ye're dead!*

Note that Maggy used broom rather than hops in her beer, and that this was thought by some drinkers to exacerbate their morning-after headaches!

The first half of the eighteenth century saw a marked growth in the number of breweries built to slake thirsts in the developing industrial areas of Scotland, and as the century progressed, Edinburgh, Glasgow and Alloa began to emerge as significant brewing centres. In 1825 there were no fewer than 29 working breweries in Edinburgh and 23 in Glasgow. Roger Protz notes that during the Napoleonic Wars supplies of Burgundy and claret were unavailable to British drinkers, so the brewing industry also expanded to capitalise on their absence during the early years of the nineteenth century.

Away from Scotland's three principal beer-making centres, most towns could boast at least one brewery by the mid-Victorian period.

Fowler's Prestonpans Brewery, 1880s

McNeill states that ale 'for centuries remained the common beverage of Lowland Scotland and the Scandinavian north-east, including Orkney and Shetland'. 'The Gael was not a drinker of ale,' she observes, and, indeed, in *Pigot's Commercial Directory of Scotland* for 1825-1826 the only brewery listed in the west of Scotland north of the Clyde estuary was that of Archibald Wright in Inveraray.

Traditionally, two main types of beer were brewed in Scotland. Scotch Ale was a strong, dark, heavy ale, which was favoured by the more well-to-do drinkers, and was colloquially known as 'nappy'. It was celebrated by Robert Burns in 'Tam o' Shanter':

> *... While we sit bousing at the nappy,*
> *An' getting' fou an' unco happy...*

The lower classes had to content themselves with Small Ale, also known as tuppenny, tippeny or tippony—as brewed by Maggy Johnstoun—which was made by mashing the spent grains from Scotch ale production a second time. Inevitably, the beer was weaker, though still probably around 4% or 5% in strength, as Scotch ale was routinely as strong as 11%. Tuppenny took its name from the price per Scots pint (about an English quart). Small ale was drunk with most meals, which was probably quite wise at a time when the average city dweller was more likely to die from polluted water supplies than from alcoholism. From 'Tam o' Shanter' again:

> *Inspirin' bold John Barleycorn!*
> *What dangers thou canst mak' us scorn!*
> *Wi' tippeny, we fear nae evil,*
> *Wi' usquabae, we'll face the Devil!'*

Captain Edward Burt in his *Letters from a Gentleman in the North of Scotland to His Friend in London* (1754) wrote of tuppenny: 'The liquor is disagreeable to those who are not used to it... the malt, which is dried with peat, turf, or furzes, gives to a drink a taste of that kind of fuel... the drink itself is apt to give a diarrhoea.'

Scotch ale was strong, smooth and usually of high quality—quite like later IPA (India Pale Ale) in character. Before its development, however, the unhopped, variable quality ales of Scotland were not held in high esteem, with many Scots who could afford to do so choosing to import English ales. In 1625 'the Hamebringing of Foreyn Beir' was banned by the Scottish Parliament in order to protect the frequently unattractive domestic product.

The heart of the problem lay in the poor quality of much native Scottish barley, and though the quality was improved during the eighteenth century, large quantities of English barley for malting purposes were imported by sea from East Anglia.

The English traveller Thomas Kirke wrote of an eighteenth-century expedition to Scotland, 'Their drink is ale, made of beer malt and tunned up in a small vessel, called a cogue. After it has stood a few hours, they drink it out of the cogue, yeast and all; the better sort brew it in large quantities and drink it in wooden queighs, but it is sorry stuff.'

Although the smaller breweries tended to have quite local markets, export of Scottish beers began at a surprisingly early stage, with England taking quantities of Scotch ale from the middle of the eighteenth century, along with the West Indies, the Baltic, and the Americas. As the British Empire expanded, countries with significant populations of expatriate Scots all became important markets for Scottish beers.

It is easy to think of aggressive brewery competition, takeovers and closures as phenomena of the second half of the twentieth century, but from the 1840s onwards the development of large-scale, urban brewing operations led to the demise of many small, and particularly rural, Scottish breweries. In 1840 Scotland boasted some 280 breweries, but by 1910 the number had fallen to 92, a decade later to 63, and only 36 remained in 1940. By 1970 the figure was down to 11.

In his short story 'The Paraffin Lamp', the great Orcadian author George Mackay Brown writes: 'He was a man who lived entirely in the past. He disliked all the fruits of progress that his fellow-islanders were beginning to splurge in: motor cars, wireless sets, gramophones, bakehouse bread, Edinburgh beer.'

As Ian Donnachie (*A History of the Brewing Industry in Scotland*) explains, 'The major transport developments of the Victorian era started the long process of concentration and rationalisation, common to Britain as a whole.'

Despite the steady numerical depletion of the Scottish brewing ranks, individual breweries grew in size, and large-scale bottling of beer became very popular during the 1920s and '30s. George Younger of Alloa and James Aitken of Falkirk were early investors in expensive bottling plant, while in Edinburgh, William Younger & Co installed bottling equipment at Holyrood in 1920 that could handle 100 dozen bottles per hour.

As subsequent pages will show, the successful production and marketing of pale ales and lagers became vital to the health of the Scottish brewing industry during the late nineteenth and twentieth centuries. Another innovation was the canning of beer, which began during the 1930s, with Tennent's of Glasgow as leading pioneers.

RATIONALISATION

Despite developments and innovations, two World Wars and sustained periods of economic recession hit the Scottish brewing industry hard, just as it did the distilling industry, and the loss of lucrative export markets during and after the Second World War only served to exacerbate the problem.

Post-war over-capacity saw many independent Scottish breweries being bought up by major English brewing companies, and some of the larger Scottish brewers joined in, too. In 1960 alone, no fewer than 10 of the 26 surviving Scottish breweries were acquired. A decade later, fewer than half of the 1960 total of working breweries were still operating.

The process of 'rationalisation' that overtook the industry during the 1960s was not a uniquely Scottish phenomenon; small firms all over England and Wales were being swallowed up by the major players at the same time. In the post-war period, output of beer in Scotland has risen dramatically, despite the equally dramatic decline in the number of companies operating in the industry, and the number of actual breweries. This has come about due to the creation of a handful of large and highly efficient units. In the early 1960s, Scottish breweries produced some 2.5m barrels per annum, but by the mid-70s that quantity had more than doubled.

According to Ian Donnachie, in the early 1950s the major players in the Scottish brewing industry were J. & R. Tennent, McEwan & Younger (Scottish Brewers Ltd) and George Younger of Alloa, followed in scale by more than a dozen companies such as Aitken (Falkirk), Arrol (Alloa), Bernard (Edinburgh), Blair (Alloa), Calder (Alloa), Campbell, Hope & King (Edinburgh), Drybrough (Edinburgh), Fowler (Prestonpans), Jeffrey (Edinburgh), McLachlan (Edinburgh), Maclay (Alloa), Murray (Edinburgh), Steel, Coulson & Co (Edinburgh), Usher (Edinburgh) and R. Younger (Edinburgh). Once the round of mergers and takeovers began, many of these long-established names disappeared in a very short space of time.

The Sunderland-based Vaux company had owned Edinburgh-based Lorimer & Clark of the Caledonian Brewery since 1919, and in 1959 they added Steel, Coulson & Co of Croft-an-Righ Brewery to their Scottish portfolio, followed shortly afterwards by the fellow Edinburgh company of Usher's. In 1961 they also bought the Perth brewery of John Wright & Co. Soon brewing was only taking place at the Caledonian Brewery and Usher's Park Brewery.

Canada's richest brewing tycoon and highly influential racehorse breeder Edward Plunkett Taylor was one of the figures who decided to turn his attention to the Scottish brewing scene, and his company Northern Breweries—which later traded as United Breweries—acquired a clutch of well-respected and long-established Scottish brewing firms, including Aitchison, Aitken, Calder, Fowler, McLennan & Urquhart, Murray and Younger. In 1962 United Breweries merged with Charrington to create Charrington United Breweries Ltd.

Native Scottish companies were not idle in the acquisitions

market either, and Tennent's bought the firms of G. & J. Maclachlan
and Turner's (Ayr) Ltd in 1960. Three years later Tennent's joined
Charrington United Breweries Ltd, trading from 1966 as Tennent
Caledonian Breweries Ltd. Scottish Brewers Ltd bought the three
Edinburgh brewing companies of T. & J. Bernard, J. & J. Morison
and Robert Younger in 1960, the same year in which they merged
with Newcastle Breweries. Also in Edinburgh, Watney Mann Ltd—
ultimately absorbed into the Scottish Courage empire—bought
out Drybrough in 1965, while Whitbread acquired Campbell, Hope
& King and John Young & Co of Musselburgh.

Once the dust had settled, only Belhaven and Maclay's remained
as independent Scottish brewing companies.

RENAISSANCE

While the brewing industry was in a state of flux, keg beers began
to make their presence felt throughout Britain, though metal kegs
had been in use since the 1930s. Putting draught beer into alu-
minium or stainless steel kegs mirrored the process of bottling beer
in many ways. It gave a uniform product that was easy to look after
and serve, and which had a comparatively long shelf-life.

Not that all drinkers saw the advantages, however, and adverse
reaction to the perceived lack of character inherent in many keg
beers developed during the 1970s, finding a focus for protest in
the Campaign For Real Ale organisation. In Scotland the reaction
against keg beer was not as pronounced as in many parts of Britain,
though a dozen small breweries dedicated to traditional brewing
methods were founded during the late '70s and early '80s.

The new 'micro-breweries' tended to be located away from the
traditional beer-making centres, and Broughton was one of the first
of the new generation of small brewing operations that sprang up.
It is the only early 'revivalist' pioneer that has survived to this day.
Broughton was founded in 1979, a year after Bothwell, which was
the first entirely new brewery to be built in Scotland since the
First World War, but sadly it lasted for less than a decade.

The survivors of the Scottish brewing renaissance are documented in the A-Z of Breweries section of this book, but many
brave ventures foundered along the way.

The early success of Broughton encouraged a number of people to follow their example, and most had the single aim of making
cask ales available once more to Scottish drinkers after decades of
neglect by the big brewers. Unfortunately for the new wave of brewers, those drinkers were not always particularly interested in being
'saved' from the products of Tennent's and Scottish & Newcastle.

Short-lived ventures included the Ayrshire Brewery at Stewarton
and the Buddon Brewery in Angus, along with operations in Buckie,
Dundee and Glasgow's Gorbals.

Other new enterprises included the Devanha, which was set up in 1982 and took its name from William Black's famous old Aberdeen brewery. The Devanha was based in the Old Station Yard in Alford and traded for a time as Aberdeen Ales after going into receivership in 1985. The brewery produced some well-regarded ales, including XB, Triple X and Pale 80/-.

Following on from the pioneering work of Bothwell in the west, Strathalbyn was developed on Clydebank Industrial Estate at Dalmuir in 1982, making Strathalbyn Original and an export beer called Strathalbyn II.

The Highlands have always been a tough market for cask ales, but Dick Saunders opened the West Highland Brewery in the former railway station at Taynuilt in Argyll and Heather Ale was brewed there for the first time in 1992. In Inverness, the Alice Brewery was founded on Harbour Road in 1983, and produced Alice Ale and a strong winter ale called Alice Sixty.

The Leith Brewery began production in 1982, and changed its name to the Argyle Brewing Company three years later. It was based in Leith's Arthur Street, and turned out a decent 80/- called Argyle 80/-. Although the Argyle brewery failed to last, Edinburgh had a long-standing, small-scale cask-ale venture in the shape of the Rose Street Brewery, based in the former White Cockade pub. The Rose Street opened in 1983, backed by the Alloa Brewing Co Ltd, and it used malt extract to produce Auld Reekie 80/- and Brewhouse Reserve. The brewery closed in 2000, following the cessation of brewing by Carlsberg-Tetley in Alloa, and Scotland lost a number of other 'brew-pubs' with the sale of the Firkin chain in 2000, as its subsequent buyer decided to cease making beer on the premises.

SCOTTISH BREWING CENTRES
Edinburgh

Edinburgh's brewing industry developed from its twelfth-century origins at Holyrood, with John Blair taking over the brewery formerly run by the monks of Holyrood in 1600. By this time, the abbey was disused, and Holyrood was a royal residence. Blair's ale met with great favour in the royal palace and far beyond.

F. Marian McNeill writes: 'By the eighteenth century, the ales of Edinburgh had won a very high reputation. One of the most popular was Bell's Beer, which was sent over a great part of Europe and even as far as the East Indies. Foreign visitors were invariably delighted with the quality of the ale, and the exiled French royalty who took refuge in Edinburgh in 1831 called the liquor "Scottish burgundy".'

It is often claimed that Edinburgh's nickname 'Auld Reekie' came about as the scale of brewing in the city grew and the reek or smell from the mashing process became a pervasive feature of the capital.

Edinburgh's development into the second largest brewing centre in Britain after Burton-upon-Trent was largely due to the quality of the water on which its brewers could draw. An underground lake—known as the 'charmed circle'—runs from Arthur's Seat to the Fountainbridge district of the city, with an offshoot running into Craigmillar, and breweries were gradually developed along much of its course. A number of wells were situated from Holyrood in the east, through the Canongate, Cowgate and the Grassmarket, to Fountainbridge in the west, and breweries were developed along the line of wells.

According to McNeill, 'The water contains a high percentage of gypsum, and it is this invaluable mineral element that constitutes the "magic" which has imparted to Edinburgh ales their distinctive quality down the centuries.'

Much as Speyside developed into *the* centre for whisky production during the late nineteenth century as it tended to produce malt whiskies that were ideal for the burgeoning blending industry, so Edinburgh's predominant role in Scottish brewing owed much to the fashion for pale ale, which grew during the late nineteenth century and early years of the twentieth century, and for which its hard water was ideally suited.

Pale ales were heavily-hopped beers with a lower strength than was common, and they were brewed principally in the east of Scotland. As the name implies, pale ales were lighter in colour than traditional Scotch ales, and they were attractive to brewers because of their shorter fermentation periods, which made for increased productivity.

Casks in yard of Maclachlan's Brewery, Edinburgh, 1920s–1940s

The Abbey Brewery, Edinburgh, from Salisbury Crags, 1880s

They also travelled well, and were therefore ideal for export markets. Indeed, India Pale Ale was brewed principally to export to far-flung parts of the British Empire.

As Edinburgh's brewing industry developed during the second half of the nineteenth century, so city centre sites left little room for expansion in many cases. The growth of the railway network also meant that brewers were attracted by the idea of being located outside the city centre, and having their own rail sidings for the import of raw materials and the export of beer.

From the 1880s onwards, brewers began to turn their attention to Craigmillar, with seven breweries ultimately being built there, though of the 36 Edinburgh breweries that were working in 1900, a dozen were located in the Canongate district of the city, and as late as the 1940s, seven still survived there.

One of the most famous of all Edinburgh brewing companies had its origins in the Canongate during the eighteenth century, and was founded by William Younger.

William Younger reputedly started work at the age of 16 in Anderson's Leith brewery in 1749. At the time, Anderson's was one of the larger Scottish breweries, turning out some 1,500 barrels of ale per year. William went on to become a prosperous excise officer, though he died in 1770 at the age of 37. In 1777 one of his sons, Archibald, set up his own brewery in the grounds of the abbey of Holyrood House, having served a brewing apprenticeship, and nine years later he also acquired the nearby Croft-an-Righ Brewery. In 1793 he opened a new brewery on the North Back of the Canongate.

Two of Archibald's brothers were also involved in brewing, and in 1784 his younger brother William began to operate his own brewery on Holyrood Abbey land. In 1803, William purchased James Blair's Abbey brewhouse and an adjacent site in Horse Wynd, next to his existing establishment, and proceeded to create a new, greatly-enlarged brewing enterprise. In 1825, however, he crossed Horse Wynd to take over a former town house, known as the Lothian Hut, which he proceeded to convert into the Abbey Brewery.

Archibald Younger died in 1819, and by the early 1820s all of the various family brewing enterprises had become unified in William Younger & Co, under the leadership of William, and successive generations of the family carried on the business down the years.

By the mid-1850s, William Younger & Co was bottling ales for export in significant quantities, and in 1859 the firm purchased Alexander Berwick's brewery, close to the Abbey, and proceeded to refurbish and re-equip it. It reopened in 1864 as the Holyrood Brewery. By 1886, Younger's were brewing 215,000 barrels of beer per annum, which was around one-sixth of the total produced in the whole of Scotland that year. The company's IPA became one of the most popular pale ales to be exported, selling all over the world during the heyday of the British Empire.

When Alfred Barnard visited Younger's Abbey Brewery he noted that it was 'planted almost at the foot of Salisbury Crags', and described it as 'one of the most ancient in North Britain'.

According to Barnard, the Holyrood Brewery was situated 'about 300 yards from the Abbey Brewery'. The total William Younger &

Holyrood Brewery, Edinburgh, 1880s

Co establishment was clearly vast, consisting of maltings in addition to the two actual breweries, and there was so much to see, and so many pieces of machinery to observe and then describe in Barnard's characteristically thorough style, that the writer spent four days on the site, while most breweries which he visited were dealt with during day trips by rail.

Whether he actually sampled it is not recorded, but Barnard noted, 'Wm Younger & Co Edinburgh Ale—a potent fluid which almost glued the lips of the drinker together, and of which few therefore could despatch more than a bottle'!

In 1921 the company's famous and enduring 'Father William' figure was created, and it became as well-known as the Johnnie Walker whisky 'striding man' logo. The character of Father William was taken from Lewis Carroll's *Alice in Wonderland*, and initially used the writer's couplet: 'You are old, Father William, the young man did say,/ All nonsense my lad, I get YOUNGER each day'.

The difficult economic times of the 1920s left few businesses untouched, not even such large concerns as Younger's and McEwan's, and in 1931 the two leading Edinburgh brewers combined to form Scottish Brewers Ltd, which in turn became part of Scottish & Newcastle Breweries in 1960 when Scottish Brewers and Newcastle Breweries merged.

By 1955, the Abbey Brewery was only being used on a seasonal basis, when extra capacity was required, and in that year the plant was closed and converted into company offices. The site was cleared during the 1990s to make way for the new Scottish Parliament. The former Park Stores bottling and kegging facility site opposite is now occupied by the Dynamic Earth visitor attraction, which is housed in the William Younger Centre.

In the early 1970s, a Harp Lager brewery, with a capacity of 350,000 barrels per year, was constructed next to the existing Holyrood Brewery. Harp Lager was jointly owned by Guinness, Scottish & Newcastle and Courage, and in 1979 the company was put into liquidation in order to allow the three partners to pursue their own lager-related ventures. Scottish & Newcastle gained the Harp lager brewery at Holyrood, the Royal Moss Side brewery in Manchester, and the right to brew and sell Harp lager through its retail outlets in return for a payment of £5m and its 32% shareholding in the Harp company. Harp Lager is currently brewed at Dundalk in the Irish Republic, and its principal overseas markets are now in the USA and Canada.

By the 1980s, Younger's famous IPA was suffering the indignity of also being marketed in cask format as McEwan's 80/-, depending on the area of distribution, while Younger's Scotch Bitter doubled as McEwan's 70/- in some outlets. Younger's Best Bitter was even brewed at the Home Brewery in Nottingham for a time

William McEwan, 1827–1913

until its closure in the mid-1990s. Today, only McEwan's 80/- survives in cask format, and perhaps the greatest loss of all Scottish & Newcastle's cask products was Younger's No. 3. This was a strong, dark, traditional beer that was brewed by the company from the nineteenth century until the 1990s, originally being known as No. 3L, as it was exported to London. Its demise was regretted by many connoisseurs of good Scottish ale.

In 1986, the Holyrood Brewery closed, bringing to an end a very long tradition of brewing in the Canongate area of the city, and the site was subsequently redeveloped for residential use.

William McEwan was born in Alloa in 1827, the son of a ship owner, and his sister married into the Younger family, of the town's Candleriggs brewery. William's uncle was John Jeffrey, who owned the Heriot Brewery in Edinburgh's Grassmarket, and William started to work there in 1851. Five years later, backed by his in-laws and with borrowed money, he set up his Fountain Brewery to the west of the city centre in Fountainbridge.

The brewery site was well chosen, being within the 'charmed circle' and close to both the Caledonian Railway line and the Union Canal, which ran from Edinburgh to Glasgow. William McEwan used the railway network to a greater extent than his rivals had previously done, and within less than two decades of starting out on his own he had created a business that was nearly as sizeable as that of the much more venerable William Younger & Co.

McEwan began to export his beers almost from the outset, taking advantage of his family's maritime connections in the process. Australia, New Zealand, the West Indies and India were principal markets for McEwan's Export and India Pale Ale, and, like William Younger & Co, the firm conducted a great deal of business with naval and military outlets.

McEwan expanded his brewery over the years, and by 1880 it covered 12 acres. When McEwan's became a limited company in 1889 it had capital of £1m. In 1973 the original plant was replaced by a completely new Fountain Brewery, which was constructed at a cost of £13m, though the landmark clock of the old brewery was retained.

The frontage of Fountain Brewery, Edinburgh, c.1910

William McEwan retired from daily involvement in the business during the late 1880s in order to further his political ambitions, ultimately becoming Liberal MP for the Edinburgh Central District in 1886, though he continued to act as company chairman. He served three terms as MP for the constituency, retiring in 1900 due to failing health.

When he died at the age of 86, William McEwan left personal assets of more than £1.5m, though he had been a most philanthropic business tycoon, gifting the McEwan Hall to Edinburgh University, and purchasing a Rembrandt for the National Gallery of Scotland.

Just as Younger's products were associated with the figure of 'Father William', so McEwan's 'cavalier' was developed from a 1930s poster series into an enduring logo, which continues to be part of the brand packaging today.

Along with McEwan's mid-century Fountainbridge development and the construction of the Caledonian Brewery on Slateford Road, two old-established brewers also moved their operations to new sites to the west of the city centre during the second half of the nineteenth century. They were John Jeffrey & Co Ltd and T. & J. Bernard & Co.

John Jeffrey had acquired the Heriot Brewery in Edinburgh's Grassmarket in 1837, though the business had been in existence for some years prior to Jeffrey's purchase. A brewery is thought to have occupied the site as far back as the sixteenth century.

By the 1860s, Jeffrey's operation had expanded to the extent that new, larger premises were required, and a site at Roseburn, on the western fringe of the city, was bought and developed during 1865/66, complete with railway sidings and a highly efficient bottling hall.

All of the actual brewing continued to be done at the Heriot Brewery until 1880, when a brewhouse was added to the Roseburn complex. The Heriot Brewery continued in production until 1900, after which the Heriot name was switched to the Roseburn site. The old Heriot Brewery in the Grassmarket has long gone, but its Victorian offices remain intact, if somewhat overwhelmed by surrounding developments.

By the early years of the twentieth century, Jeffrey's operated a sizeable estate of tied houses, and had an extensive export trade. The company also became a significant player in the expanding lager market, adding a lager brewery at Roseburn in 1902, and taking on the former Tennent's lager brewer Jacob Klinger.

During the 1950s, John Jeffrey & Company Ltd brewed ale and stout for James Calder & Co Ltd, after Calder's regular contract brewers, Archibald Arrol & Sons Ltd, converted their Alloa Brewery to produce only lager. Interestingly, this echoes

Heriot Brewery, Edinburgh, 1980s

the arrangement in existence today, whereby the Caledonian Brewery—not far from the site of the Heriot Brewery at Roseburn—contract-brews Calder's products for the brand's owner, Carlsberg-Tetley.

In 1960, Jeffrey's business was acquired by Northern Breweries Ltd, and while a number of other acquisitions were closed down, the Heriot Brewery was subsequently expanded, with some brands of Fowler's, Murray's and George Younger's beers being brewed there. Ultimately, the brewery became part of Tennent-Caledonian Ltd, and a kegging line was installed in 1967. From 1969, Bass Export and Bass Special were brewed there, and a decade later a new lager brewery was built. Just four years after this, however, the bottling line was closed, and 'rationalisation' brought about the closure of the entire plant in September 1992. During the late 1980s Heriot was producing 45,000 barrels per year, and was making lagers for the Tennent's range. Today, the brewery is lost beneath a residential development.

Alfred Barnard visited T. & J. Bernard & Co's old Edinburgh Brewery on the North Back of the Canongate, but noted, 'During the last two or three years Bernard's Edinburgh Ale has been in such great demand that the firm found it absolutely necessary to build this year the other and larger brewery at Gorgie.'

This was an imposing structure located between Gorgie Road and Slateford Road, which opened in 1888 and was initially known as the New Edinburgh Brewery. Soon after Barnard's visit,

Bernard's New Edinburgh Brewery, late 1890s

production at the Canongate brewery ceased. The firm's successful expansion was largely due to the efforts of John Mackay Bernard, son of the founder of the original Edinburgh Brewery. In 1960, Bernard & Co was acquired by Scottish Brewers Ltd, shortly before their company's merger with Newcastle Breweries.

While Jeffrey's and Bernard's moved west, other brewers opted for Duddingston and Craigmillar to the east. The first brewer to set up in the area was William Murray, who arrived in Edinburgh in 1886 from near Kelso in the Borders. He was soon followed by Andrew Drybrough & Co, whose Craigmillar Brewery opened six years later. Subsequently, Pattison, Elder & Co, Blyth & Cameron, T. Y. Paterson & Co and W. & J. Raeburn all constructed breweries in the area. Finally, in 1902, the Glasgow company of G. & J. Maclachlan built the Castle Brewery. In a period of 16 years, seven new breweries had been created in one square mile of land.

The firm of Drybrough & Co Ltd had its origins in the first half of the eighteenth century, when Andrew Drybrough was a baker and brewer, initially based on Tolbooth Wynd, off the Canongate. James Boswell (1740-95) was said to be an enthusiastic imbiber of Drybrough's ales when he was living in James Court, Edinburgh. Around that time, Bell's Brewery in The Pleasance was a large-scale operation, and the place where, in the opinion of Hugo Arnot, writing in his *History of Edinburgh* in 1779, 'the best strong beer is made of any brewed for sale in Scotland'. In 1782 the Drybrough business was relocated to a less cramped site on the nearby North Back of Canongate, and during the 1870s it expanded to a second brewery on the opposite side of the road, formerly the home of Steel, Coulson & Co.

Railway development in the area curtailed any further expansion, however, and brought about Drybrough's move to Craigmillar. In 1885 the firm became a limited liability company, trading as Drybrough & Co Ltd, although full control remained with members of the Drybrough family.

Drybrough's survived as an independent entity until 1965, when it was effectively taken over by Watney Mann Ltd, who proceeded to invest heavily in the site. By this time, Drybrough's Craigmillar Brewery was the only one still operating in the area. In 1967 the adjacent former North British Brewery was purchased and the brewhouse was subsequently demolished to make way for kegging and bottling facilities.

More than £1m was also spent upgrading and doubling the capacity of the actual brewing plant, with further expansion taking place in the early 1970s, by which time Watney Mann Ltd had itself become part of the Grand Metropolitan Group. The brewery concentrated on producing keg and canned beers, including Drybrough's Keg Heavy—first introduced in 1952—and Best Scotch.

In addition to Keg Heavy and Best Scotch, during its twilight years Drybrough's also brewed Burns Ale, the cask ale Pentland, and Private Reserve, a rare and highly-regarded beer that was only available in bottles. In 1984 Drybrough's 80/- was launched as a 'real ale', selling alongside Pentland 70/-, and the company's cask ale sales increased dramatically as a result.

Early in 1987, Grand Metropolitan sold Drybrough & Co to the Alloa Brewery Co Ltd, and as the Alloa Brewery was already

Drybrough's workforce, Edinburgh, 1923

running considerably below capacity, the new owners proceeded to close the Drybrough facility immediately, though the Drybrough brand name lived on for a short time.

Today virtually all traces of brewing and malting have disappeared from Craigmillar, though in late 1999 brewing made a welcome return to the district when the Fisherrow Brewery opened at Duddingston Yards. The Fisherrow takes its name from Whitelaw's long-lost Fisherrow Brewery.

If Drybrough's could claim to be the last of the old Craigmillar-based brewers, then the Pattison brothers of the Duddingston Brewery must surely deserve their own place in the record books for the spectacular nature of their company's collapse.

The Pattison brothers, Robert and Walter, are synonymous in whisky circles with the great distilling boom of the late nineteenth century. They were noted for their flamboyant advertising, opulent lifestyles and, ultimately, for the creativity of their accounting methods. Both brothers served prison terms for fraud, and the collapse of Pattison's Ltd in 1899 sparked the end of 'boom' and the onset of 'bust' in the Scotch whisky industry.

It is less well known that the Pattisons were also Craigmillar-based brewers. They showed questionable taste by producing a blended whisky to commemorate the death of General Gordon at Khartoum in 1885, but their beer marketing also tended to leave much to be desired. One advertising slogan ran:

North, south, east, west
Pattison's Ales are the best.
East, west, north, south,
Pattison's Ales in every mouth.

Following the collapse of the Pattison company, the Newcastle upon Tyne brewers Robert Deuchar Ltd acquired the almost-new Duddingston Brewery for the knock-down price of £25,000. Robert Deuchar was originally from Fife, and his desire to purchase the Duddingston Brewery was based on the popularity of Edinburgh pale ales in the north-east of England, where the water available for brewing was not well suited to their production.

In 1900, Robert Deuchar Ltd also bought the business of Simson & McPherson Ltd, who had operated St Mary's Brewery near the Canongate since 1864. Deuchar's subsequent actions were to be repeated all too frequently in the Scottish brewing industry, as St Mary's Brewery was closed as surplus to requirements, and Simson & McPherson's Abbey Brewery in Melrose soon suffered the same fate.

In 1953, Newcastle Breweries Ltd bought the Robert Deuchar business, and three years later took over the firm of James Deuchar Ltd, set up by Robert Deuchar's younger brother. Among the assets of James Deuchar Ltd was the Lochside Brewery in Montrose.

Lochside Brewery/Distillery, Montrose, 1990s

Lochside looks as though it would be more at home in Munich rather than on the Scottish east coast, as it was built during the 1890s in uncompromisingly Germanic *brauhaus* style. It was constructed on the site of an eighteenth-century brewery, drew water from its own artesian wells, and had the brief distinction of being the only brewery outside Newcastle to produce Newcastle Brown Ale, with two freighters making regular trips from Montrose Basin to the Tyne with cargoes of 'Broon'.

Once in the ownership of Newcastle Breweries Ltd, Lochside was closed, and in 1956 was sold to Macnab Distillers Ltd. It was converted into a distillery, and much of the brewing plant was removed, though the copper-lined brewing vats remained in place. Lochside produced whisky until 1992, latterly under the ownership of Spanish company D. Y. C., who were ultimately absorbed into the Allied Distillers empire. At the time of writing, the abandoned distillery remains as a distinctive feature in the Angus landscape, but it is unlikely to avoid demolition and site redevelopment for much longer.

The merger of Newcastle Breweries Ltd and Scottish Brewers Ltd in 1960 left the new company with greater brewing capacity in Edinburgh than it needed, and Duddingston ceased production in 1961. The brewery, which was the largest of the seven located in the Craigmillar and Duddingston area, was demolished during the early 1970s.

Another famous Edinburgh brewing name was that of Usher's. The company of Thomas Usher & Son Ltd had its origins in a firm founded by James Usher in 1831 in a brewery in Chambers Street, though as business grew a new brewery, named the Park, was built in St Leonard's Street in 1860. During the 1890s, one of the company founders, Thomas Usher, bought out his nephews after a major policy disagreement, and began to trade as Thomas Usher & Son Ltd.

Usher's was acquired in 1960 by the Sunderland brewer Vaux, who proceeded to invest heavily in the Park Brewery. In 1980, however, Vaux sold the Usher operation to Ind Coope, who closed the Park Brewery and switched production to their Alloa plant.

Two other well-known Edinburgh brewing operations, those of Campbell, Hope & King and Young's of Musselburgh, were both acquired by Whitbread & Co in 1968. Three years later, brewing ceased at Campbell, Hope & King's eighteenth-century premises in the Cowgate, where Archibald Campbell had started brewing in 1740. The former 'grand hall' and hops store of the old brewery have now been incorporated into the Tailor's Hall Hotel and Three Sisters pub complex. Young's brewery was closed in 1969 and subsequently demolished, with the site being developed for residential use.

Glasgow

For many years, Glasgow was Scotland's second 'brewing city', with more than 20 operational breweries in the early nineteenth century. Glasgow boasted a much softer water supply than its rival to the east, and this softer water was ideally suited to the production of porter and, later, of stout.

Porter was made with roasted, unmalted barley and had a high hop content. It required several months of maturation before sale, but it had the advantage that its production could utilise hops and malt that were not of the highest quality.

Initially porter was imported to Scotland by sea from London, but by the 1750s modest quantities were being produced in Edinburgh, and in 1762 the Anderston Brewery was established in what was then a village close to the city of Glasgow. This was the first significant porter brewery in Scotland, and it engaged a London porter brewer by the name of Nathaniel Chivers, who also instructed John Struthers of the Gallowgate Brewery.

Not only was Glasgow's water well suited to the brewing of porter and stout, but the influx of Irish immigrants to the west of Scotland in the second half of the nineteenth century ensured a ready market for the product. The public appetite for porter was, however, widespread, and during the nineteenth century the drink was being brewed in places as far apart as Dumfries and Aberdeen.

Around 1745, John Crawford built a brewery outside the Glasgow city boundaries in Grahamston, and when it was offered for sale in 1760, the Grahamston Brewery was described as 'sufficient for carrying on an extensive business in brewing strong ale, small beer, twopenny, and whisky… [It] may likewise be rendered fit for making porter.'

In 1778 the Anderston Brewery was advertising 'common porter' for sale at £2. 8/- per hogshead (a barrel containing approximately 55 gallons), and 'best porter', which had been matured for more than a year, at £3. 4/- per hogshead. The company boasted that it was 'not inferior to the London brown stout'.

Other major Glasgow breweries that were established during the late eighteenth and early nineteenth centuries included William Scott's Barrowfield Brewery, Ebenezer Connal & Sons' Finnieston Brewery, Hugh Baird's Great Canal Brewery, and Robert Struthers' Greenhead Brewery.

Stout was easier to produce than porter, and required less maturation time, and during the final three decades of the nineteenth century it came to eclipse porter throughout Britain. However, stout itself was soon overtaken in popularity by pale ale, while Scottish brewers were also increasingly preoccupied in producing a drink called lager.

British lager is commonly thought of as a phenomenon of the later twentieth century, but bottled lagers from Denmark and Germany were available in Scotland in limited quantities by the 1880s, and sales grew as drinkers began to develop a taste for lighter coloured and lower-strength beers.

The first lager to be brewed in Britain was produced by Edinburgh-based William Younger & Co, who began to experiment from late 1879 at their Holyrood brewery, using a Danish strain of yeast from the Carlsberg brewery. Younger's ultimately decided to concentrate on producing pale ales, however, but Tennent's began to brew lager in Glasgow in 1885, and went on to establish a worldwide reputation for the product.

The Tennent family were originally farmers from Cumbernauld who moved to the northern outskirts of Glasgow, where they combined farming with market gardening and traded as maltsters and brewers. Documents show that in 1556 Robert Tennent was a private brewer and maltman based near Glasgow Cathedral, and in 1776 the firm of J. & R. Tennent set up in business as public brewers and maltsters in rented premises on a site in the Drygate area, now incorporated into the company's present Wellpark complex. The following year J. & R. Tennent were able to buy the premises, and by 1793 were prosperous enough to purchase the neighbouring

Wellpark brewery, too. Wellpark Brewery is the only Glasgow firm listed in Tait's commercial directory for 1783 which remains in the same line of business, trading from the same site more than two centuries later.

The area where the Tennents began to brew ale had a distinguished brewing heritage, almost certainly dating back to the time in the twelfth century when monks began to build Glasgow Cathedral on the site of St Mungo's grave. In the mid-thirteenth century, Dominican and Franciscan monasteries were founded in the district and, like most monastic orders, the Dominicans and Franciscans were consummate brewers. Brewing activity in the area was centred around the Molendinar Burn, which was a source of high-quality water.

At Christmas 1745 the Jacobite troops of Charles Edward Stuart stopped at the Wellpark brewery for food and drink, with the city records stating that 'each and every man was refreshed and heartened by the brew'. A decade later, Robert Tennent built the Saracen's Head, Glasgow's first high-class hotel, which subsequently became the city's principal coaching inn. Among its illustrious patrons were Robert Burns, William Wordsworth, Dr Johnson and James Boswell.

As Robert Tennent and his brother John prospered, their brewing site was expanded to take in the neighbouring establishment of William McLehose in 1793, giving the firm a five-acre spread. Four years later the first record of company exports occurs, with a shipment of Scotch Ale being dispatched from the Clyde to thirsty expatriate Scots in America and, in particular, to Scots in Virginia, who were supplying tobacco to Glasgow factories. The strength of Scotch Ales was so great that they could be transported on long sea voyages without any deterioration in quality. By the middle of the nineteenth century, Tennent's were the largest exporters of ale in the UK, and their products also proved popular south of the border, with consignments being sent by sea to Bristol and Liverpool.

Robert Tennent died in 1826, and John survived him by just a year. Control of the company subsequently passed to Robert's eldest son, Hugh, who ran it for the next 28 years, during which time Tennent's became the world's leading exporter of bottled beers. Around this time, the brewery's cellars could hold 80,000 barrels of ale, ranging in size from the standard hogshead to 600-barrel stout vats.

By the 1880s, Tennent's were major employers, with their own stabling, a cooperage, sawmill, and even a printing works for producing labels on-site. The company owned the Possil Pottery, which produced stone 'jacks', ideally suited to export markets as they were less fragile than bottles. The pottery also produced ceramic advertising items.

Hugh Tennent's grandson, also Hugh, suffered from poor health, and in 1881-82 he spent time in Europe, touring health spas. While there, he sampled Bavarian lager beers, which he then proceeded to introduce to Wellpark Brewery. Concern had already been expressed that the growth of continental lagers was threatening Tennent's lucrative export market for pale ale, so it seemed a logical step for the company to begin lager brewing itself.

Just as London porter brewers had been employed to establish its production in Scotland, so a German lager brewer by the name of Jacob Klinger and a Dane called Eric Westergaard were engaged to supervise the new venture. The theory was that together they would combine the best features of German and Danish lagers. Production began in May 1885, and so successful was it that four years later a complete lager brewery was constructed alongside the existing ale brewery.

Tennent's new lager brewery was built to full German specifications, and German coopers were even employed to make the distinctive 20-barrel and 40-barrel cellar casks that were required for lager maturation. These 'great casks' had to be sufficiently airtight to prevent the escape of carbon dioxide produced by secondary fermentation, as a comparatively high level of carbonation was an important stylistic feature of the new product.

The methods of producing lager and traditional Scotch ale were surprisingly similar, with soft water being ideal for both. Many of the techniques associated with lager production had long been used at Wellpark to produce a 'keeping' beer suitable for export, and it has been suggested that Scotch Ale was really a kind of dark lager, hence, perhaps, the fact that Scottish drinkers embraced lager more

Tennent's Well Park Brewery, 1890s

Wartime female workers at Tennent's Wellpark Brewery, Glasgow 1916

readily than those in many parts of Britain during the 1960s and '70s.

One of the earliest celebrity customers for Tennent's lager was 'Buffalo Bill' Cody, whose 1892 Wild West show in London was supplied with the drink.

Despite the scepticism of the Glasgow press, which dubbed the lager brewery a 'madman's dream', lager production enabled Tennent's to survive through the difficult trading times of the early twentieth century, though sadly Hugh Tennent did not live to see his brainchild achieve its full potential. He died in 1890, aged just 27, and was the last member of the family to be in direct control of the company.

Following the successful development of lager brewing, Tennent's continued to be innovative, introducing beer cans during the 1930s. The cans used initially were short and stubby, and would have looked more suitable as containers for metal polish. According to many palates, they also tainted the beer. In 1955 the company launched a flat-topped, 16-ounce or 'two-glass' can, which had to be pierced with two holes in order to pour the product, and which was the true forerunner of the modern 'ring-pull' beer can.

From 1957 the cans carried views and even recipes, before the introduction of the famous 'lager lovelies' in 1962. The first girl to be featured was the model Ann Johansen, who was pictured beside a fountain in Trafalgar Square. Such was the enthusiastic response to Ann by lager drinkers that she featured in a complete series of adverts, and during the next two decades many young 'lovelies' pouted seductively from the side of Tennent's lager cans.

In 1963 the company began to market draught lager. According to one school of thought, once draught lager was available in bars the product finally shed its image as a 'woman's drink', and the great growth in male lager consumption in Scotland began.

According to Donald Carswell, writing three decades earlier in *The Scots Weekend* (1935), 'Glasgow manufactures a special light lager of which even the Germans speak with a reverence verging upon awe and not unmixed with envy. But there is no home market for it. If you want to taste it you must ship yourself somewhere east of Suez.' How times change!

During the great rush of rationalisation and consolidation

Tennent's 'lager lovelies'

in the brewing industry during the early 1960s, Tennent's acquired their Glasgow rivals Maclachlan's, and also Turner's Ayr & Newton Breweries, with whom they had enjoyed trading links since 1934. Maclachlan's Castle Brewery had been founded in Maryhill in 1889 by George and John Maclachlan, a pair of brothers originally from Perthshire, who in 1901 opened a second Castle Brewery in the Craigmillar district of Edinburgh. Along with Maclachan's brewing business, Tennent's also gained the Lowland whisky distillery of Auchentoshan, located at Dalmuir, near Clydebank.

In 1963 Tennent's became a subsidiary of Charrington United Breweries Limited, and in 1966 they formally merged with United Caledonian Breweries (C. U. B.'s second Scottish holding) to form Tennent Caledonian Breweries Ltd. The following year, Tennent Caledonian became part of the Bass Charrington Group—subsequently Bass plc—who continued to own it until they divested themselves of their brewing operations in 2000.

Over the years, and particularly as the popularity of lager rose dramatically during the 1960s and '70s, much of the original Wellpark Brewery has disappeared during progressive programmes of redevelopment and expansion. Vast stainless steel fermenters and large cellar tanks were installed during the late 1970s, and in

1984, no doubt to the consternation of some committed drinkers, new plant was installed to produce non-alcoholic Barbican!

In 1900, Glasgow had boasted no fewer than 14 breweries, but only Tennent's survived beyond the Second World War, thanks largely to their diversification into lager production. Brewing restrictions during the First World War helped to kill off a number of Glasgow breweries, particularly as the restrictions were not applied in Ireland, allowing Guinness, Beamish & Crawford and Murphy's to corner the market in stout production. The gradual change in public taste away from porter and stout towards the pale ales of Edinburgh and Alloa also did little to help the cause of Glasgow brewers.

John Struthers' Gallowgate Brewery survived for longer than most of its fellow Glasgow brewing companies, moving to a site near Glasgow Green, where it became known as the Greenhead Brewery and continued trading until the 1930s.

For many years, Tennent's could boast that it was Glasgow's only brewery, but in 1994 the Glaschu Brewery opened in a former car showroom on Woodlands Road, supplying the Uisge Beatha bar next door with Pride of the Clyde and Keely Light ales. Sadly, its demise came about two years later, when local residents complained about the smell of brewing. Tennent's Glaswegian 'micro-rivals' now include Miller's Thumb and the Clockwork Beer Company.

Alloa

The Clackmannanshire town of Alloa once boasted eight working breweries, and it owed its prominence in the Scottish brewing industry to a number of factors. There was a ready supply of locally available barley and coal, and suitable water from the Ochil Hills, not to mention an efficient transport link by the River Forth to London and other markets. The Forth also provided an entry point for English malting barley. During the later eighteenth and early nineteenth centuries, Alloa found itself at the centre of a developing industrial area, which meant that there was also a strong local market for ales in addition to sales opportunities further afield.

When he visited George Younger & Son's Candleriggs and Meadow Breweries while researching the second volume of his *The Noted Breweries of Great Britain and Ireland* (1889-91), Alfred Barnard described Alloa as the 'Burton of Scotland'. He wrote that Alloa Ale was 'renowned in Scottish song and held in high repute in distant lands'. He also noted that the first reference to ale brewing in Alloa dated from 1645.

> *Awa' wi black brandy, red rum, and blue whisky*
> *An' bring me the liquor as brown as a nut;*
> *O! Alloa Ale can make a chiel frisky,*
> *Brisk, faeming a' fresh frae the bottle or butt.*

from *Alloa Ale* by John Imlah (1827)

Candleriggs Brewery, Alloa, 1880s

In 1762 George Younger had set up what was almost certainly the first commercial brewery in Alloa, purchasing a property that contained a malt kiln and loft for the purpose. Two years later, Younger bought adjoining buildings from Robert Stein, a member of the renowned brewing and distilling family, and the two sites subsequently became the Meadow Brewery.

Candleriggs brewery was founded in 1787-88 by Robert Meiklejohn, and leased to Younger's in 1852, the year in which Meiklejohn & Sons purchased the Grange Brewery. In 1871, Younger's bought Candleriggs Brewery, and six years later brewing ceased at the Meadow, with the site eventually becoming company offices.

Much of Younger's increasing business was with export sales, and large quantities of beer were being shipped to the West Indies and Australia by the middle of the nineteenth century, with South Africa and India subsequently becoming important markets too. By the time of Barnard's visit, Candleriggs Brewery was turning out up to 25,000 barrels of ale per year. Younger's was the third-largest Scottish brewing company after the Edinburgh duo of William Younger and William McEwan.

During the 1880s, the trade in bottled beer grew dramatically, particularly for export, and Younger's bottling department was moved from Candleriggs, in the centre of Alloa, to Kelliebank, close to the River Forth, where the first chilling and carbonating plant in Scotland was installed in 1903. The carbonated beers produced there proved extremely popular in both domestic and export markets. By 1912 the Kelliebank site was too small to cope with demand, and a new Home Bottling Department was created at the Eglinton Dye Works. Kelliebank became the Export Bottling Department, and the Forth Brewery is now housed in one of the surviving bottling halls, which dates from 1884.

Younger's had its own cooperage and maltings and, from 1908, the company even made its own bottles. The present glass works, close to the Forth Brewery at Kelliebank, had its origins in Younger's bottle-making operation.

Barnard noted that 'The change in the popular taste from heavy strong ale to the light and more sparkling beverage, was quickly taken advantage of by Messrs G. Younger & Son. Anticipating the demand, in an incredibly short time, they had succeeded in placing their East India pale and bitter ales in the foreign markets, until they were in such demand as to necessitate an extension of the premises.'

Younger's success also led them to County Durham and the purchase of Fenwick's Sunderland Brewery and the Chester Brewery in Chester-le-Street in 1898, while in their home town they bought the Grange Brewery in 1919. Finally, 40 years later, they acquired Alloa's Townhead Brewery. Shortly afterwards, however, the family-run Younger's company was taken over by United Breweries. Candleriggs Brewery closed in 1963, and its site, adjacent to Maclay's now silent Thistle Brewery, is a public car park.

Staff of Blair's Townhead Brewery, Alloa, 1920s

If George Younger and Robert Meiklejohn were pioneer Alloa commercial brewers, others were not slow to follow in their footsteps. The Alloa, Forthbank, Hutton Park, Mills and Shore breweries were all founded during the first two decades of the nineteenth century, while Robert Knox's Forth Brewery had been established at the nearby small port of Cambus in the late 1780s or early 1790s.

By 1845 the town's eight breweries were turning out a total of some 80,000 barrels of ale per annum, and when Barnard visited more than half a century later there were still eight working plants in the town. These were the Alloa, Candleriggs, Caponcroft, Grange, Mills, Thistle, Townhead and Shore breweries, while the Forth in Cambus continued in operation. By the time of George Younger & Son's demise during the early 1960s, the tally of Alloa's breweries consisted of just their Candleriggs operation, Maclay's Thistle Brewery, and Ind Coope's Alloa Brewery.

Archibald Arrol, 1815-88

Archibald Arrol was a Stirlingshire-born, Glasgow-based wine and spirits merchant, who worked in partnership with Archibald Tower. In 1866 Arrol purchased the Alloa Brewery, founded in 1810 by a consortium that included Andrew Roy. Arrol's company had been West of Scotland agents for 'Roy's Alloa Ales', so this diversification into brewing was a logical step. Under Arrol's control, the Alloa Brewery was expanded significantly, and the business traded as Archibald Arrol & Sons Ltd until 1951. In that year, Ind Coope and Samuel Allsopp of Burton upon Trent assumed full control of the business, and decided to brew only lager. Three years later, the brewhouse was rebuilt, incorporating Swedish equipment.

The Alloa Brewery's link with lager production had begun in 1921, and came about largely due to the involvement of John Calder. Calder was born in 1867, the second son of a well-to-do Alloa timber merchant who had purchased the town's Shore Brewery in 1862. Under John Calder's control the brewing business thrived, trading as James Calder & Co Ltd from 1905. Such was Calder's entrepreneurial expertise that he also managed the struggling Burton brewery of Samuel Allsopp & Co from 1913, turning

The Shore Brewery, Alloa, 1880s

its fortunes around in impressive style, and somehow finding time to run Archibald Arrol & Sons Ltd, too.

Calder closed the Shore Brewery in 1921, and contracted out his company's brewing requirements to Arrol's. In the same year, lager-making equipment was transferred from Allsopp's defunct High Street Brewery in Burton upon Trent to the Alloa Brewery, along with Swedish-born lager brewer Joseph Lundgren. Lager brewing plant was also purchased from Belgium, and installed at Alloa. In 1927, the Alloa Brewery introduced a new lager, called Graham's Golden Lager, which proved enormously successful, and in the late 1950s was rebranded as Skol.

In 1930, Allsopp & Co obtained a controlling interest in Arrol's, who had been supplying them with lager for several years, and four years later John Calder was responsible for orchestrating a merger between Allsopp & Co Ltd and their principal Burton rivals, Ind Coope & Co Ltd.

By 1960, Calder was a wealthy man with diverse business interests, and in that year he sold James Calder & Co Ltd to Northern Breweries Ltd, and the company's identity was soon lost. He died two years later at his estate in Perthshire, aged 94. Today, the Calder name survives, principally in a range of keg ales brewed for Carlsberg-Tetley by the Caledonian Brewery in Edinburgh.

A year after Calder's death, the Alloa Brewery became part of Allied Breweries when that company was created from Tetley Walker, Ansells and Ind Coope. More than £2.5m was invested in the Whins Road site during the 1980s and '90s, but this still could not prevent its closure in 1998 as part of what were by that time Carlsberg-Tetley's rationalisation plans.

Carlsberg-Tetley's Alloa Brewery, 2000

Latterly, beer-making was reintroduced alongside lager production and, from 1982 until shortly before production ceased, the Alloa Brewery continued to use the Arrol name for its cask ales, which by then consisted of 70/-, 80/- and an occasional brewing of 90/-. Archibald Arrol's 80/- enjoyed a good reputation as a malty, fruity heavy, even earning a plaudit from CAMRA's *Good Beer Guide*, which described it as 'well worth seeking out when in top form'.

Today, Carlsberg-Tetley continues to use the Alloa site for adminstration and distribution purposes, but the brewery is silent, and the illuminated 'SKOL' sign has been taken down from the tower, leaving just a ghostly outline of lettering on the brickwork.

SOME OTHER FAMOUS NAMES
Aberdeen: William Black & Co

As befits a long-established, major population centre with a busy harbour trade, Aberdeen was for many years a significant location for brewing, with 22,700 barrels of various ales and porters being produced in the city and its environs in 1811. Thirteen Aberdeen breweries are listed in *Pigot's Commercial Directory of Scotland* (1825-26), including William McBean's Aberdeen Brewery in Meal Market Lane, William Black & Co's Devanha Brewery, the Gilcomston Brewery Co, the New Bridge Brewery, Ferryhill Brewery, and Smith, Irvine & Co of Old Aberdeen. In the county of Aberdeenshire, two breweries were listed as operating in Peterhead and one in Inverurie.

The oldest of the commercial Aberdeen breweries recorded by Pigot was the Gilcomston Brewery, which was founded in 1767, a year before the Devanha, which became the largest brewery operating in northern Scotland. The Devanha was constructed on a site to the north-west of the River Dee, and, in addition to its local custom, also exported strong ale and porter by sea. In return, the brewery received cargoes of Norfolk barley from 1807 onwards. In his 1818 *Annals of Aberdeen*, William Kennedy wrote that the Devanha Brewery 'has acquired great celebrity for the excellence of its porter, not only in the town but in Edinburgh, Glasgow and other places. The porter of this brewery is frequently exported to London, where it finds a ready market.' The brewery took its name from the area of the 'Granite City' in which it was located, and its owners built the Devanha Distillery close by in 1837.

According to Alfred Barnard (*The Whisky Distilleries of the United Kingdom*, 1887) 'the Government resolved, about the year 1820, to encourage distilling under legal authority, and the erection of Distilleries was suggested to the brewers of the period. Strathdee, one of the first Distilleries in Aberdeenshire, was erected by Mr Ogg, the principal partner of the Ferryhill Brewery, and about the same time the Devanha Distillery was established by the owners of the brewery of that name.'

Government statistics for 1841 record that there were 58 brewers and 36 maltsters resident in Aberdeen, though by the early 1870s there were only three medium-sized breweries operating in the city. The last to survive, the Devanha Brewery, succumbed to the economic depression of the inter-war years.

Blackford: R&D Sharp Ltd

Blackford in Perthshire was one of the few rural Scottish breweries to be visited by Alfred Barnard, who wrote:

From a very remote period, the brewery at Blackford has been noted for the excellence of its ale, which is attributed to the fine character of its wells, and the peculiar adaptation of their waters for brewing purposes. It is remarkable, that, although the wells of the premises of the Blackford brewery are quite close to each other, their waters are so distinct in their character, that two of them are highly suitable for the production of pale and sweet ales, and a third for porter brewing.

The brewery is said to be the oldest in Scotland, but this has been disputed by some historians, who claim for the Banff brewery the honour of being the very first public brewery ever erected in Scotland; and fix the date very soon after the middle of the fifteenth century... There is scarcely any doubt the Sharp's brewery (whose product has been praised in prose and song) is built on the foundations of the ancient brewhouse referred to.

You'll find out what you've come in search of here;
Tankards that hold half-pints of Blackford humming beer.

Barnard continues, 'The brewery which presents a neat and lofty elevation, is constructed of red sand-stone, and, with its tall shaft and prominent buildings forms the most striking object in the valley'. When Barnard visited Blackford, the former brewhouse, built in 1610, was still standing, and being used as a beer store.

The site of the Blackford Brewery is now occupied by Tullibardine distillery, and a number of breweries and brewery locations across Scotland subsequently became centres for whisky-making. Both crafts require a guaranteed supply of pure water and, in the days before road and rail networks were developed, comparatively local sources of barley, coal or peat were also essential. Perhaps the most famous distillery to be based on an old brewery is Glenmorangie at Tain in Easter Ross. 'The fine character of its wells' has ensured that Blackford's water continues to be highly prized, and the village is now home to the world-famous 'Highland Spring' operation.

In 1897 a new brewery opened in Blackford to compete with Sharp's enterprise, and according to the *National Guardian* for 20 August of that year, 'Blackford Brewery is erected on the site of the late Mr Eadie's old establishment... A siding is to be brought from Blackford Station into the brewery, thereby doing away with all cartage to the station.'

The Blackford Brewery was owned by the long-established Perth company of W. B. Thomson, who constructed 'a large factory for the manufacture of aerated waters' next to the brewery. Thomson's already owned the North British Mineral Water Works in Perth, and, according to the *National Guardian*, 'In addition to brewing beer and manufacturing aerated water, the firm are large bottlers, extensive blenders, and do a considerable retail trade. They are possibly the largest beer and stout bottlers in Scotland north of the Tay.'

The Blackford Brewery, Perthshire, 1880s

Dundee: Hugh Ballingall & Son

When Alfred Barnard was researching his epic *The Noted Breweries of Great Britain and Ireland*, Ballingall's was a sufficiently prominent venture to tempt him to visit Dundee. He wrote: 'From Dundee Law we overlooked Mr Ballingall's breweries and could see the busy movements in that hive of industry.'

Barnard also quoted from the 1822 book *Dundee Delineated* to the effect that 'at one period there was not a town in Scotland where brewers were more numerous or ale more famous, than in Dundee... For some time past, from the change of manners in the place, and from the great taxes paid on malt and wort to Government, the brewers are diminished in their numbers, and the strength of the diminution in the number of brewers may be attributable in part to the extensive brewery in the Pleasance which has been long and successfully carried on.'

The Pleasance Brewery in Hop Street had been in existence since the mid-eighteenth century, and by the time it came into the hands of Dundee Provost and businessman William Ballingall in 1844 it had caused many of the city's brewing rivals to fall by the wayside, as the author of *Dundee Delineated* suggests.

When William Ballingall died in 1856 he was succeeded by his son, Hugh, and direct family involvement in the business continued for more than a century. Under the control of Hugh, Ballingall's grew dramatically, with output increasing twelve-fold between 1850 and 1890. The Pleasance Brewery was extended to cope with demand, but in 1880-81 an impressively appointed new brewery, christened The Park, was constructed on the opposite side of Hop Street to supplement its output.

Ballingall's Pleasance Brewery, 1880s

Ballingall's new Park Brewery, Dundee 1880s

Barnard noted: 'The indomitable perseverance and industry deployed by Mr Ballingall, has resulted in his building up a business which has no rival in the north of Scotland.' He continued: 'The firm's reputation is based upon the superior quality of their Scotch pale ales, which are sold all over the North of England and throughout Scotland.'

By the time of Barnard's visit to Ballingall's, only the Craigie Brewery, the King Street Brewery and the Victoria Brewery existed as Dundee rivals, along with William Gray & Son's Fort Street brewery in nearby Broughty Ferry.

Gray's range of ales was extremely popular in the city of Dundee and throughout the counties of Forfarshire and Angus. The firm had been founded in 1846 and survived until 1923. The Craigie Brewery remained in business for a further six years, before succumbing to the prevailing economic depression, leaving Ballingall's as Dundee's only brewing company.

Barnard sampled a number of Ballingall's beers and was obviously impressed, because, whether writing about distilleries or breweries, he rarely mentions the taste of the product, no matter what exhaustive detail he goes into concerning the capacity and external dimensions of the production plant. He noted that 'The firm's special brand of pale ale, which was exhibited at the Paris Exhibition, is certainly as delicious as any we have tasted. Without being heady, it is highly nutritious, bright and sparkling, and tastes well of the hop.'

In addition to its domestic trade, Ballingall's also had a thriving export business, most notably for its pale ales and porter, with markets that included America and Australia. Much of the export trade failed to survive the First World War, however, and the local market was badly hit by recession in Dundee's principal source of employment, the jute industry. Dundee also became a bastion of the Temperance Movement, which did nothing to increase sales.

In 1960, the last Ballingall family member to be involved in the business, Hugh, great-grandson of the founder, retired as chairman. By that time, the Pleasance Brewery was no longer working, and the Park Brewery was operating well below its optimum level of output. Markets had become very localised and, in 1964 Ballingall's came to an arrangement with Drybrough & Co whereby the Edinburgh company would brew and bottle all of the Dundee firm's requirements.

In February 1968 a decision was taken to wind up Hugh Ballingall & Son, as sales of cask and keg beer had declined for several years. At the time, Ballingall's was the most northerly operational brewery in Britain. The brewery buildings were demolished during the 1970s, and the site is now part of an industrial estate.

Falkirk: James Aitken & Co

While touring Scottish breweries, Alfred Barnard visited Aitken's of Falkirk, one of the country's leading brewers and exporters at the time. Aitken's specialised in overseas markets during the second half of the nineteenth century, and the brewery was extended in 1866 and again twelve years later, while the company's maltings at Linlithgow were enlarged in 1875. For many years, the Edinburgh & Union and the Forth & Clyde canals were utilised to transport Aitken's products to Edinburgh and Glasgow.

Barnard wrote:

> From a remote period this establishment has been noted for the quality of its brew, several writers having mentioned its product as 'good and excellent ale'. During the last half century, the foreign business has rapidly increased owing to the high-class beer brewed by this enterprising firm. Their trade is principally export, and they are holders of several prize medals, among them being one for Sydney International Exhibition, 1879, Melbourne 1880, and another for Calcutta, 1883-4 etc...
>
> Real merit inevitably attracts recognition sooner or later, and therefore it is not surprising that a product so excellent as Aitken's beer and so wholesome and refreshing, should have become the standard drink in Australia and the colonies. This success is attributed not only to the quality of the beer, but to the cleanly, perfect, and careful nature of the bottling.

Aitken's had been founded in 1740 and remained in family ownership for some 200 years, closing in the mid-1960s after its

Aitken's Brewery, Falkirk, 1880s

acquisition by Northern Breweries. The Lint Riggs brewery is still remembered in Central Scotland for its advertising slogan 'Strength Behind Bars', which featured a caged tiger.

Perth: John Wright & Co

It is recorded that a brewery was in existence on Perth's North Methven Street in 1786, though it is thought that brewing could have been taking place there from the beginning of the eighteenth century.

One of the brewery's founders was William Wright, who was succeeded in the business by his nephew John Wright. After John's death in 1895, the business was acquired by a banker, Robert Nimmo, and the Alloa brewer R. B. Wallace.

A late-Victorian advert for Wright's noted: 'A unique feature of the establishment is an artesian well which for well over One Hundred Years has given a supply of pure, pellucid water for Brewing and Aerated Water purposes.' Originally situated in the brewery's grounds, on land once owned by Blackfriars Monastery, this well was later hidden beneath a new bottling hall, though it continued to supply the brewery with process water.

By 1900, Wright's were brewing their own range of beers, and were also bottling Guinness and Burton ales, as well as cider, under licence. In 1926, the company purchased its only surviving Perth rival, Muir & Martin's South Inch Brewery, which dated from 1815. During its twilight years in the late 1950s, Wright's products included Heavy and Light draught beers, along with a range of bottled beers which included Brown Ale, Export Ale, Pale Ale, Strong Ale and Sweet Stout.

Wright's Perth Brewery, 1950s

In September 1961, the *Perthshire Advertiser* announced the purchase by Vaux & Associated Beweries Ltd of John Wright & Co (Perth) Ltd, noting, 'The staff and employees of Wright & Co are being retained. There are between 50 and 60 full-time workers at the firm's brewery in North Methven Street, Perth, and the figure is brought up to nearly 100 by those employed by subsidiary companies and in just over a score of licensed premises controlled by Wright's in Perth city and county and neighbouring shires.' Chairman Sir Robert Nimmo made the point that the business was financially sound, 'and added that the brewery output was at its highest level for over ten years'.

This did not, however, prevent Vaux from closing Wright's brewery within a short time of its acquisition, concentrating their Scottish production in Edinburgh. Wright's Brewery complex survived until the 1980s, when it suffered the fate of so many other old urban breweries, with the buildings being demolished and the valuable site subsequently redeveloped for housing.

ARRAN

*Arran Brewery, Cladach Visitor Centre, Brodick,
Isle of Arran KA27 8DE*
www.arranbrewery.co.uk
***tel**: 01770 302353* ***email**: info@arranbrewery.co.uk*

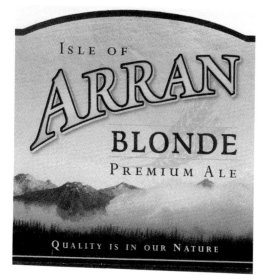

Until recent years, the Isle of Arran had lacked any legal alcohol production since the last distillery at Lagg closed in 1837, but it now enjoys the luxury of both a modern distillery at Lochranza, opened in 1995, and a brewery.

The Isle of Arran Brewing Company began production in February 2000, and is located in the hamlet of Cladach, close to Brodick Castle and in the shadow of Goat Fell. It is operated by Richard Roberts, a former sculptor from Buckinghamshire, and his Glasgow-born wife, Elisabeth. Richard oversees the brewing process, ably assisted by Dan Goronwy and a skilled and enthusiastic team of staff. Richard attended a number of brewing courses, researched the subject extensively, and gained work experience in two breweries during the six years while the Arran project was being developed.

According to Richard, 'We chose Arran because we loved the place and wanted to live here, but also because most of the real ale developments seem to have been away from the West of Scotland, further east, and we thought that gave us some scope. Another important factor is that the Arran name and image is very marketable. People associate it with quality produce.'

Arran is a purpose-built micro-brewery with a walk-through viewing gallery, tasting room and gift shop, and its 20-barrel plant was purchased virtually unused from the Townhouse brew-pub in St Helier on Jersey. It then spent the best part of two years in storage before being installed in its new, considerably more northerly island home. The brewery is laid out on two floors, with the mash tun situated on the level above the copper and the fermenters.

The project cost some £600,000 to develop, and currently brews between 30 and 40 barrels per week, though there is the capacity to produce up to 100 barrels per week if required. The brewery is equipped with its own two-head bottling line, which can handle up to five barrels in one bottling session. At the end of 2000, some 75% of output was being sold in cask format, but it is anticipated that the level of bottled sales will rise during the next couple of years.

Cask Arran ales are available in more than 50 hotels and bars throughout Scotland, and more is actually sold in Edinburgh than in the West of Scotland. Bottled Arran ales are stocked by a wide range of specialist outlets around the country, and in England Waitrose offers Arran ales in some 70 supermarket branches. In late 2000, the brewery enjoyed its first export sales to Japan. While the brewery handles sales on Arran and in the Kintyre area itself, EPM (tel: 0141 6440900) processes all other orders.

During the brewery's first year in production it won 'Best Beer' awards at two festivals. Arran Dark took the top spot at the Paisley Beer Festival, while Arran Blonde was successful at the Ayrshire Beer Festival. The brewery has also won an award for its distinctive bottle labels.

The brewery visitor centre is open 9.00 am to 5.00 pm seven days per week during the tourist season, and reduced hours during the winter months, when it is closed on Sundays. Bottled beers are available on a mail-order basis from the brewery, along with a range of branded goods and other items of Arran produce, including the island's excellent malt and blended whiskies.

ARRAN BLONDE (5.0%)

Pale gold in colour, continental-style beer, well-balanced and hoppy on the nose and palate. Available in cask and bottled formats.

ARRAN DARK (4.3%)

Fuller-bodied, more malty and hoppy than Arran Light, with a smooth texture and a deep, dry finish. A traditional Scottish heavy. Available in cask and bottled formats.

ARRAN LIGHT (3.8%)

Bronze-coloured, refreshing, creamy bitter with a perfumed hop aroma and a nice flavour balance of fruit and hop. Available in bottled format, and marketed as **Arran Ale** *when on draught.*

AVIEMORE

The Aviemore Brewery Co Ltd, Unit 12, Dalfaber Industrial Estate,
Aviemore, Inverness-shire PH22 1PY
tel: *01479 812222* **fax:** *01479 811465* **email:** *aviemore.brewery@dial.pipex.com*

The Aviemore Brewery Co Ltd was set up by former aircraft engineer and keen amateur brewer Norman Swinton in late 1996, though he is now no longer involved with the company. Production began in September 1997, with the Ruthven Brew—the first of the so-called Wolfe of Badenoch range. The Wolfe of Badenoch was Alexander Stewart, a son of King Robert II, and during the fourteenth century, the Wolfe terrorised Strathspey from his home in Ruthven Castle, burning Elgin Cathedral in 1390.

The brewery has a ten-barrel plant, and brewing takes place up to six times per week. A bottling line was installed in November 1997, which can process up to 500 bottles per hour, though crowning and labelling are performed manually. According to the brewery, annual output and sales are still growing, and some 80% of Aviemore's production is sold in cask format, which is against the trend for many Scottish breweries of similar size, which have concentrated on bottling at the expense of cask sales.

Aviemore Brewery sells and delivers casks direct to a wide range of outlets in Scotland, including pubs in Glasgow, Edinburgh and the Borders. Because the beer can be delivered by van the same day as it leaves the brewery, the quality of the product on tap is high. Aviemore has a marketing link with **Carlsberg-Tetley** and the **Caledonian** brewery, which gives its cask ales access to many more outlets. Casks are sold into England through agents, and have penetrated as far south as Brighton.

Bottled Aviemore beers are sold in free houses and specialist retail outlets throughout Scotland, but they may well be more widely available in the future. The Whisky Shop in Dufftown on Speyside stocks Aviemore ales, and offers a mail order service, including mixed cases from a variety of Scottish breweries (tel/fax 01340 821097; email: *whiskyshop.dufftown@virgin.net*). Because the present bottling line lends itself to short runs, Aviemore is happy to produce personalised bottlings for clients in comparatively small quantities, and will also supply personalised casks, complete with individual pump-clips.

At present, Aviemore Brewery occupies a site with little scope for expansion, but the company is on the lookout for a new location in or close to the popular holiday destination of Badenoch and Strathspey, where a new complex could be constructed, incorporating a pub and visitor centre, in addition to the brewing plant itself. A more state-of-the-art bottling line would probably be a feature of any new development, though it is thought unlikely that the brewery would opt to increase the actual brewing capacity from the present level of 10 barrels.

In August 2000, the Aviemore Brewery hosted the 'Thunder in the Glens' Harley-Davidson motorbike rally, complete with a Wolfe of Badenoch look-alike contest. The prize for the most convincing Wolfe was a holiday in Milwaukee, the home of Harley-Davidson (and US brewing giant Miller). A limited edition of Hogswill (HOG = Harley Owners' Group) in cask and in bottles was also produced and bottled especially for the rally. Continuing the slightly unlikely 'biker' theme, the brewery was one of the sponsors of the 'Superbike' championship event at Knockhill racing circuit near Dunfermline.

In 2000, Aviemore acquired many of the assets of the **Tomintoul** brewery from the Offical Receiver, and with the addition of Tomintoul's 20-barrel plant and site, along with some popular and well-regarded Tomintoul brands, Aviemore has become the largest micro-brewer in Scotland.

Brewery tours are available by appointment between 9.00 am and 4.00 pm, Mondays to Thursdays, and between 9.00 am and 1.00 pm on Fridays.

CAIRNGORM BREW (4.5%)
A refreshing, golden-coloured beer that combines Scottish malt and continental hops. Available in bottled format only.

CAIRNGORM GOLD (4.5%)
Cask version of Cairngorm Brew.

HIGHLAND IPA (3.6%)
A crisp, fresh-tasting light ale, available in cask format only.

MURDOCH (4.8%)
A strong, copper-coloured ale. Malty, nutty, full-bodied and quite dry. Available in 500ml bottles.

RED MURDOCH (4.8%)
330ml bottled version of Murdoch.

RUTHVEN BREW (3.8%)
Satisfying, malty, hoppy, copper-coloured ale, available in cask and bottled formats.

SHEEPSHAGGERS GOLD (4.5%)
330ml bottled version of Cairngorm Gold, also available with this name in casks.

WEE MURDOCH (4.8%)
Cask version of Murdoch.

BELHAVEN

Belhaven Brewing Company Ltd, Spott Road, Dunbar,
East Lothian EH42 1RS
www.belhaven.co.uk

tel: 01368 862734 *fax*: 01368 869500 *email*: info@belhavenbrewery.demon.co.uk

Brewing has taken place in the coastal town of Dunbar, some 30 miles from Edinburgh, since Benedictine monks sunk wells and dug storage vaults at Belhaven some time before the sixteenth century. The Benedictine order was noted for its brewers, and King David I of Scotland had gifted the Isle of May in the Firth of Forth to Benedictine monks in 1150. From May, they began to colonise areas of Fife and the Lothians, and they were subsequently granted lands at Bele harbour, near Dunbar, later to be known as Belhaven.

During the 1550s, the now secular Belhaven Brewery supplied ale to the Franco-Scottish army that had been assembled at Dunbar Castle, in readiness for an invasion of England.

Remarkably, two Benedictine wells and the vaults survive, and are incorporated into the present brewery, which has the date 1719 carved into a lintel. It is recorded that in the early eighteenth century, the brewery was owned by John Johnstone.

Belhaven is the oldest working brewery in Scotland and one of the oldest in Britain. It combines traditional methods with modern technology, and the compact brewhouse is equipped to produce cask ales, keg ales and lager. The company is the largest regional brewer north of the Border, and Belhaven is the third-largest brewery in Scotland. The brewery has been upgraded and extended progressively during the past two decades in order to increase capacity, and in 1991/92 a bottling hall was installed, where kegging, bottling and packaging now take place under one roof.

Although there has been no on-site malting since the 1970s, 'listed' malt kilns from 1719 are still *in situ*, and there was a time when Belhaven Brewery supplied not only its own malt requirements, but also those of several local distilleries. All malt used by Belhaven is Scottish in origin, with the Chariot variety currently being favoured.

That great biographer, lawyer, man about town and drinker James Boswell described the produce of Belhaven as 'the finest small beer I ever tasted in my life', and a man with Boswell's capacity—for many things—should surely have had plenty with which to compare it.

In 1827 Belhaven Brewery was able to place an advert in the London *Morning Chronicle* proudly stating that the Austrian Emperor had chosen Belhaven ale for his cellar, and that he had called it 'the burgundy of Scotland; and famed as Bavaria is for its strong beer, it cannot produce the like'. As early as the 1830s, Belhaven ales were available in London, where the company had appointed an agent.

Belhaven still uses the 'burgundy of Scotland' quote in its advertising material for 80/- cask ale, and Robert Disher & Co of the Edinburgh & Leith Brewery hijacked the slogan a century and more ago, applying it to their popular and highly potent Disher's Ten Guineas Ale.

For 250 years the brewery at Belhaven was owned by the same family, and traded as Dudgeon & Co. Sandy Hunter acted as the last family Chairman and Head Brewer, before the company was sold to a hotel group in 1972. Hunter, now in his eighties, continues to live in retirement in a splendid house situated close to the brewery.

During the first two decades following its sale, Belhaven experienced some chequered times, changing hands several times. 'Colourful' owners included Miss World promoter Eric Morley and the Polly Peck businessman Asil Nadir. In 1993 a management buy-out gave the company much-needed stability and self-confidence. Belhaven remains one of the very few independent Scottish survivors of the passion for amalgamation and rationalisation that swept through the British beer industry from the early 1960s onwards.

Belhaven now has a total capacity of around 100,000 barrels per year, and currently produces almost 75,000 barrels, whereas in 1992 the figure was around 30,000 barrels. Belhaven has a strong reputation for its cask ales, so it comes as something of a surprise to discover that cask beers now account for just 5% of total output, though the company's commitment to producing traditionally brewed real ale remains undiminished.

Some 45,000 barrels per year are sold in bottled format, of which

80% is contract work. Tennent's Lager, which accounts for 55% of all bottling work undertaken, is brewed at Wellpark in Glasgow, and tankered east to Dunbar. Tennent's Sweetheart Stout is also bottled and packaged by Belhaven.

All Whitbread Pale Ale sold in Scotland in bottled form is both brewed and bottled under contract by Belhaven, while the company also brews and bottles beers for a number of small Scottish breweries. Since the closure of the Thistle Brewery, Belhaven has produced all of **Maclay's** keg and bottled ales, and the super-market giant Asda is another important customer.

Belhaven Brewery supplies the 110 tied houses owned by the 'Belhaven Pubs' trading division, along with some 1,400 other outlets. In addition to the main brewing plant, Production Manager and Head Brewer George Howell, who formerly worked for Tennent's at their now-demolished Heriot Brewery in Edinburgh, set up a five-barrel brewing operation for experimental purposes in April 1999.

A recent innovation was the installation of a reverse osmosis plant, formerly used by the now closed Vaux brewery in Sunderland. This removes nitrates from water, and has enabled Belhaven to revert to using well water from wells originally dug by the Benedictine monks, rather than paying large sums of money to take water from the mains supply.

Draught and packaged beers are exported to 14 countries, with the USA being a principal market. Belhaven also sells in Canada, Australasia, Germany, Italy, Switzerland and Scandinavia. Scottish Ale (the equivalent of 80/-) is brewed exclusively for the export market, and is canned for Belhaven by Guinness.

Occasional cask-conditioned guest beers are issued, and in the past these have included Christmas Cracker, Festival, Five Nations, Fayre Ale, Le Jaggy Bonnet (brewed for the World Cup), Rudolph's Revenge and Special Cargo.

Tours may be arranged, and the visitor reception area/bar features fascinating photographs and artefacts relating to the brewery's past. A range of branded merchandise and bottled beers is also on sale.

BEST (3.2%)

A well-balanced, smooth, honey-coloured ale with a tight, creamy head, delivered on draught by a mix of carbon dioxide and nitrogen (commonly known as 'nitrokeg'). Excellent session beer for non-real ale drinkers. Also available in 'Draughtflow' cans. One of only two Belhaven products available in can, Best is canned for the company by Whitbread plc. Since its introduction in 1990, 'Best' has become a major revenue-earner for Belhaven and, ironically, to some extent has probably supported the continuation of cask beer production. The company describes Best as 'our star performer'.

BEST EXTRA-COLD (3.2%)

Chilled to 6°C at the point of dispense, Extra-Cold was one of the first draught ales to be produced in response to the perceived demand by Scottish drinkers for colder draught beers.

EXPORT (3.9%)

Robust, distinctive export with a bitter-sweet palate. Mixed gas delivery.

80/- (4.0%)

Malty on the nose and palate, while the hops give quite a tart aspect to its flavour. Toffee and nutty in character, with a long, dry, fruity finish. Placed second in the 1997 Champion Beer of Scotland awards. Available in cask and bottled formats.

HEAVY (3.9%)

Medium-bodied heavy with carbon dioxide delivery.

HURLY BURLY (4.5%)

Oat malt stout, rich and characterful, very dark and almost chewy. Available in cask and bottled formats.

IPA (4.0%)

Clean, sharp and bitter. A good example of the style. Available in cask format.

LIGHT (2.7%)

Dark and refreshing, very drinkable. Mixed gas delivery.

90/- WINTER ALE (8.0 %)

Strong ale, which shares toffee and nutty characteristics with its 80/- cousin, but is also decidedly fruity. Full-bodied, rich and warming. Only available seasonally on draught, but is also bottled at 6.5%.

ROBERT BURNS SCOTTISH ALE (4.2%)

Characterful Scottish ale, malty and well-balanced. Originally brewed by Tennent's in 1996 to commemorate the bicentenary of the great bard's death. After a year, however, the brand passed to Belhaven, who had previously undertaken its bottling because the volumes being produced were too small for Tennent's to continue with. Available in bottled format.

Scotland's national bard has, quite appropriately, given his name to several beers over the years, including a popular Strong Ale brewed by Drybrough & Co Ltd.

SANDY HUNTER'S TRADITIONAL ALE (3.6%)

Stylistically, a typical Belhaven beer, in that it is malty and nutty. Hops, malt and sulphur dominate on the nose, and there is a distinctive bitter-sweet flavour.

ST ANDREWS ALE (4.9%, bottled at 4.6%)

Notably hoppy in aroma and flavour, fruity, with peppery notes too. Full-bodied, with a bitter aftertaste. The beer gets its name from the fact that the flag of St Andrew magically appeared in the sky during a battle between the English and the Scots near Dunbar, and the Scots subsequently won. Also available in keg format (4.4% mixed gas delivery).

SCOTTISH LAGER (4.1%)

Crisp, clean and refreshing flavour. Carbon dioxide delivery. Also available bottled.

70/- ALE (3.2%)

Honey-coloured, malty beer, hoppy and fruity, with a sulphur-like nose, in common with the 60/- and 80/-. Sweet and nutty, with a light finish. Also available bottled.

60/- PALE ALE (2.9%)

A rare Scottish mild ale with a distinctive roast character, walnut-brown in colour. Brewed to an old Scots recipe. A CAMRA Beer of the Year in 1996, 1999 and 2000. Also available bottled at 2.6%.

BLACK ISLE

Black Isle Brewery, Old Allangrange, Munlochy, Ross-shire IV8 8NZ
www.blackislebrewery.com
tel: 01463 811871 *fax*: 01463 811875 *email*: djg@blackislebrewery.com

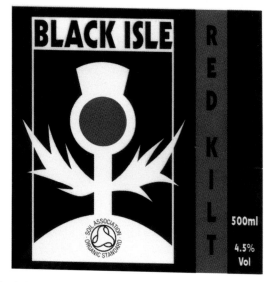

The Black Isle Brewery was founded in 1998 by David Gladwin, and is based in a converted farm buildings at Old Allangrange on the Black Isle, six miles from Inverness. During renovation work on the house, an old bottle seal bearing the name of 'Allangrange' was discovered, suggesting that a brewery of some sort had operated there in the past.

According to David Gladwin, who originally hails from Somerset, but has lived and worked in the Black Isle area for the past two decades, 'We're surrounded by malting barley here, so it seemed sensible to make some good, local beer. I'm a great believer in regionality. If I go to Inverness, for example, I don't want to drink London beer, I want something brewed locally.'

Inverness was once a significant brewing centre, due to the local availability of good barley, and Guild & Wylie's Thornbush Brewery and Buchanan & Company's Haugh Brewery survived until the early 1900s. There were also commercial breweries in the towns of Cromarty and Tain, and the famous Glenmorangie distillery at Tain was formerly McKenzie & Gallie's Morangie Brewery. Before the advent of the Black Isle Brewery, an attempt to revive brewing in the area took place with the development of the small-scale Alice Brewery in Inverness, which operated during the 1980s.

Black Isle is a five-barrel brewery that produces an average of 15 barrels per week, and cask sales tend to be within a 50-mile radius of Inverness, with the emphasis being on local customer loyalty. Black Isle has its own bottling line, and David Gladwin notes 'brewing, bottling and labelling are all done on site, we don't contract anything out'.

In December 2000, the Black Isle Brewery purchased the Plough Inn, situated in the nearby Moray Firth coastal village of Rosemarkie. 'It's one of the oldest commercial buildings on the Black Isle,' says David, 'and was built in 1691. Red Kite will be permanently available, and our other beers will be on offer from time to time too. In summer, we'll have three or four different pumps on the go.'

The brewery's Red Kite is available in bottled format through Scottish branches of Safeway, and it is anticipated that in future the supermarket chain may take other brands and extend its range of Scottish bottled beers to its English branches. The full bottled Black Isle range is also to be found in many specialist outlets throughout Scotland.

David Gladwin now produces three organic beers, made using hops and malt that have not been treated with artificial fertilisers or preservatives. 'I believe there is definitely a place in the market for organic beer,' he says. 'Then not only can people enjoy a drink but they can do it with a conscience, knowing they are doing their bit for the environment.' As though most of us needed an excuse…

In late 2000, the brewery produced the first of its range of 'specials', namely 5.0% Hibernator, a naturally cloudy organic wheat beer. The 'special' will be changed regularly, and during the summer it is likely that there will be a new one every month.

Black Isle beers are available by mail order from the brewery as well as online, and the brewery shop is open from 10.00 am to 6.00 pm, Monday to Saturday. It is well signposted from the A9 north of Inverness. Brewery tours are available.

GOLDEN EAGLE (3.8%)
A sweetish, 70/- style amber-coloured beer, malty, with a bitter finish and lots of character for its strength. Cask format only, Golden Eagle is available during the winter months, and alternates with Yellow Hammer.

GOLDENEYE IPA ORGANIC ALE (4.0%)
Refreshing, golden, pale ale, bitter and hoppy. The use of American Cascade hops gives a citrus, grapefruity flavour. Bottled format only.

GREEN KILT (4.8%)
Bavarian-style organic lager, introduced during 2000. Bottled format only.

RED KILT (4.5%)
Organic version of Red Kite, introduced during 2000. Bottled format only.

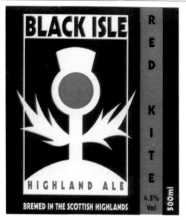

RED KITE (4.5%)

A traditional 80/- style beer, bright amber in colour, with an aroma of oranges and an attractive nutty flavour. Well-balanced and refreshing. Available in cask and bottled format.

THORNBUSH PORTER (4.8%)

Named after a long-lost Inverness brewery, Thornbush Porter is a dark, rich brew with a fine, creamy head, made with a complex blend of pale chocolate malts, black malts and oats. Available in bottled format only.

WAGTAIL (4.5%)

Ruby-red in colour, with roast malt and fruit notes, and a satisfyingly dry finish. Available in cask format only.

YELLOW HAMMER (4.3%)

Pale summer ale, with strong citrus and hop notes on the nose and palate. Attractive bitter finish. Available in cask format only, Yellow Hammer replaces Golden Eagle during the summer months.

BORVE BREW HOUSE

Ruthven, Huntly, Aberdeenshire AB54 4SG
tel: *01466 760343*

Borve Brew House was established on the Isle of Lewis in 1983 by Borve House hotelier James Hughes and his brewer son, Gregory, using equipment from the Penhros Brewery. Initially, one barrel per week was produced for the family hotel, and a number of other local outlets were subsequently served. The market for real ale in the Hebrides was always going to be very small, however, and the Hughes's could ruefully claim that they sold more beer in Manchester than they did in the whole of the Outer Hebrides.

In 1988 the operation was transferred to a former school at Ruthven in the Grampian foothills, where the brewery and a Brewery Bar were developed.

In 1995 Aberdeenshire Ales joined Borve among the ranks of Aberdeenshire brewers, and their Buchan Gold was produced from a converted farm steading at Drumwhindle, near Ellon. Sadly, the venture proved short-lived. The brewing copper was fabricated by the Rothes firm of Forsyth & Sons, whose handiwork more usually graces the still houses of Speyside distilleries.

Borve is one of the more idiosyncratic Scottish brewing operations, and goes out of its way to avoid publicity. By the first half of 2000, beer-making had been temporarily suspended.

Usually, Borve ales in bottled format are offered through a number of specialist retailers in the Grampian region, and draught versions have a similarly limited local currency. Export sales have been strong in Finland and Italy, while past products have included Cairm Porter, made with liquorice.

BORVE ALE (3.9%)
Reddish-brown in colour, a Scots ale with a hoppy aroma and a rich, malty flavour. Available in cask and bottle-conditioned formats.

EXTRA STRONG ALE (10.0%)
Very highly regarded smoky and hoppy strong ale, with a nose of apples. Partially fermented in casks that have previously contained bourbon or Scotch malt whisky. Available only in bottle-conditioned format.

TALL SHIPS IPA (5.0%)
Classic IPA style, hoppy and refreshing. A cask and bottle-conditioned ale which has been produced since 1991.

BRIDGE OF ALLAN

The Brewery, Queen's Lane, Bridge of Allan, Stirlingshire FK9 4HP
www.bridgeofallan.co.uk
tel: 01786 834555 *fax*: 01786 832065 *email*: brewery@bridgeofallan.co.uk

The Bridge of Allan Brewery is a modern, purpose-built structure, created by proprietor Douglas Ross in 1997 behind the Queen's Hotel in the Victorian spa town of Bridge of Allan, near Stirling.

Douglas spent 25 years in the licensed trade before finding that his ale-brewing hobby was taking up almost as much time as his 'proper' job of running the Queen's Hotel, and he subsequently sold the hotel in 1999 to concentrate full-time on brewing. Also in 1999, the brewery's attractive and interesting visitor centre opened to the public.

The brewery turns out some 15 barrels per week, giving an annual production of around 800 barrels. 70% of sales are currently of cask ales, and 30% of bottled beers.

The Bridge of Allan Brewery Company owns two pubs, the Railway Tavern in Dollar and the Real Mackay in Kilsyth. The brewery distributes directly to some 50 outlets in Central Scotland, but its beers are available through wholesale distributors as far south as Exeter, while Safeway stocks bottled Bannockburn ale. Products from the Bridge of Allan and **Sulwath** Breweries are also available via the Bridge of Allan website.

The Bridge of Allan Brewery is one of two breweries that currently make up Scotland's Craft Brewers' Cooperative, the other being **Sulwath** in Castle Douglas. The co-operative originally also embraced the **Valhalla** Brewery in Shetland, and Chris Lynas' Lugton Brewery in North Ayrshire, though that has now closed, and the site of the Lugton Brewery and Inn has been sold for housing development. The Bridge of Allan Brewery has, however, acquired some plant from Lugton, and the rights to brew John Barleycorn, Lugton Gold and Millennium Ale.

Bottling used to take place at the Lugton Brewery, but Bridge of Allan beers destined to be sold in bottled format are now tankered to Castle Douglas in Galloway on a regular basis for bottling on the Sulwath line.

Douglas Ross initially named his beers after battles fought in the vicinity, but as the range of products has expanded, even Central Scotland's warlike history has been unable to offer enough conflicts, though the 'Battle Pack', consisting of a bottle of Bannockburn, Sherrifmuir and Stirling Brig is a popular seller.

The Bridge of Allan Brewery gained national media exposure when Douglas Ross launched Wee Jocky's Chicken Ale in the spring of 2000. 'Jocky's' is brewed using eggs, which Douglas claims echoes a sixteenth-century recipe for Cock Ale, though without the unpalatable bits of poultry included in the original. He also claims that it prevents hangovers, due to the proteins, vitamins and minerals present in eggs.

Douglas Ross managed to turn potential embarrassment to good publicity when he announced the launch of Euro 2000 Ale as an 'occasional beer' in anticipation of Scotland qualifying for the football tournament. The team failed to qualify, but the brew was produced anyway, and again the media were happy to tell the story.

A wide range of seasonal and occasional brews is produced, with the former including—in chronological order—Spring Ale, Summer Breeze, Harvest Ale, Wheat Beer and Sporran Ale Winter Warmer. A particular favourite is Bronwyn Festive Blonde Ale, which is brewed at Christmas, and features the Ross family's Golden Retriever bitch on its pump clip, complete with 'Santa' hat!

Bridge of Allan Brewery also undertakes a wide range of corporate and personalised bottlings.

Entry to the micro-brewery and adjacent visitor centre is free of charge, and opening times are 10 am to 5 pm, seven days a week, all year round. Free samples are available, and group tours are possible by arrangement.

BANNOCKBURN (5.0%)

Light-coloured and refreshing. Launched in May 2000 in bottle-conditioned form due to its success as a draught ale, and the most heavily promoted of the Bridge of Allan range.

BEN NEVIS-WEST HIGHLAND WAY CRAFT ALE (4.0%)
Along with Glencoe and Lomond Gold, Ben Nevis is one of Bridge of Allan's three organic cask products, launched late in 2000. A fully-flavoured, ruby-coloured beer, considered by Douglas Ross to be 'very morish'.

BRAVEHEART (4.8%)
A bottle-conditioned beer, only available at the brewery shop from the summer of 2001.

E-BEER (5.0%)
Described by Douglas Ross as 'the first beer of the internet', e-Beer is only available online.

GLENCOE ORGANIC STOUT (4.5%)
A dark, fully-flavoured, malty traditional stout, made using organic oats.

JOHN BARLEYCORN (5.0%)
Formerly produced by the Lugton Brewery. Heather honey is added to give this ale a notably smooth taste.

LOMOND GOLD ORGANIC CRAFT LAGER (5.0%)
Fully-flavoured traditional lager, with lots of fruit on the palate and a long aftertaste.

LUGTON GOLD (5.0%)
Another former Lugton Brewery product preserved by Douglas Ross. Marketed as 'Scotland's tastiest lager'.

SHERRIFMUIR (4.5%)
A ruby-coloured bitter ale, only available in bottled format.

STIRLING BITTER (3.7%)
Popular draught session ale, pale in colour and with a light aroma, yet fully-flavoured and quite bitter, with a nutty, fruity taste and a dry, refreshing aftertaste.

STIRLING BRIG (4.1% draught, 4.8% bottle-conditioned)
A traditional Scottish 80/- ale, which was the inaugural beer of the brewery, and remains its best-seller. The brewery was founded in the year of the 700th anniversary of the battle of Stirling Brig (1297), when the forces of William Wallace defeated the English army at Stirling, hence the beer's name. Available on draught and also in bottle-conditioned format.

STIRLING DARK MILD (3.2%)
Very drinkable, lightly-hopped mild or 'light' ale, brewed using a high percentage of dark and chocolate malts. Stirling Dark Mild has a deep, creamy head, while malt and roast flavours predominate. Available in draught format only.

STIRLING IPA (4.2%)
A full-bodied draught IPA with characteristic hoppy nose, strong malt flavour and a clean, bitter finish.

WEE JOCKY'S CHICKEN ALE (4.4%)
The presence of egg yolk gives the ale its distinctive colour, and also adds to the flavour. Originally a one-off brew for the Railway Tavern in Dollar, Chicken Ale proved so popular that it is now established as a regular part of the Bridge of Allan range.

BROUGHTON

Broughton Ales Ltd, Broughton, Peebleshire ML12 6HQ
www.broughtonales.co.uk
tel: 01899 830345 *fax*: 01899 830474 *email*: beers@broughtonales.co.uk

Broughton Brewery is situated in the Scottish Borders, just off the A701 Moffat to Edinburgh road, and five miles from Biggar. The brewery was one of the earliest of the 'new wave' of small-scale Scottish breweries, being founded in 1979 by David Younger and James Collins, who were keen to resurrect Scotland's almost-defunct cask-brewing tradition. David Younger is a member of the seventh generation of the famous Edinburgh brewing dynasty, and a former Scottish & Newcastle executive, while James Collins is a member of the equally famous Scottish publishing family.

Broughton is one of the few breweries dating from the early days of the Scottish real ale revival to remain in business, though it has not all been plain sailing for the company. A year prior to the establishment of Broughton, Tom Abercrombie had opened the first entirely new Scottish brewery since before the First World War at Bothwell in Lanarkshire, where he brewed Bothwell Heavy. Sadly, the venture failed to survive a decade, and it was just one of many comparatively short-lived new brewing ventures that sprang up in the wake of Broughton's initial success. (See Heritage section.)

A 40-barrel brew-plant was installed in the former village sheep abattoir in order to brew Greenmantle Ale, giving a weekly capacity of more than 200 barrels. The original brew plant is still in use, having been added to and upgraded over the years. In August 1995 Broughton went into receivership, but was subsequently acquired by Giles Litchfield, who had opened his Whim Ales brewery in Derbyshire two years previously. The new Managing Director injected capital into the newly created Broughton Ales Ltd, and increased the availability of Broughton beers through a network of wholesalers. Giles Litchfield lives locally, and is involved in the running of the brewery on a day-to-day basis.

Annual output at Broughton is around 5,000 barrels, 70% of which is now sold in bottled format, and 14 staff are employed. According to Brewing Director Alistair Mouat, who moved to Broughton six years ago after serving at Belhaven Brewery for 20 years, the proportion of bottled beer has increased from 50% of total output when he arrived at the brewery. A few years prior to that, bottled sales only accounted for some 30% of throughput. Bottling is undertaken by Robinson's of Stockport, who also handle bottling requirements for the Borders' other brewery at **Traquair**.

Some 200 Scottish outlets are supplied directly from Broughton, and wholesalers, including the Beer Seller, distribute Broughton ales in both cask and bottled formats further afield. All the major supermarket chains are stockists, along with Victoria Wines and Oddbins, and the John Lewis Partnership is one of the three leading outlets for Broughton's bottled range, selling significant numbers of their presentation gift packs.

Beers are exported to the USA, Canada, Japan, Scandinavia and a number of countries in mainland Europe, and the brewery anticipates a significant level of growth in the US market during the next few years.

Broughton produces a number of 'regular' seasonal ales each year, including Winter Fire, First Foot, Bramling Cross and Northdown. The most idiosyncratic of the seasonals is, however, Reekit Yill. The name comes from the Lowland Scots for 'smoked ale', and Reekit Yill is brewed using a percentage of peated malt, which makes its presence known in the finished product. This is a very elusive cask ale, with only a dozen or so barrels being brewed each January. It was originally produced to commemorate the bicentenary of Robert Burns' death in 1996, and has been made annually ever since.

Broughton also brews Discovery Ale, a 4.2% light, refreshing, golden ale which celebrates the centenary in 2001 of the launch of the ship RRS *Discovery*, the vessel that carried Captain Scott and his party to Antarctica and which is now on display in its home port of Dundee.

Brewery tours can be arranged for groups, and beer may be purchased from the brewery during office hours. Broughton has also recently started to sell its products online.

BLACK DOUGLAS (5.2%)

A dark-red, strong, winter ale, named after Sir James Douglas, who had strong associations with the Broughton area, and was a friend of Robert The Bruce. Douglas carried Bruce's heart into battle during the Crusades. Available in draught and bottled formats.

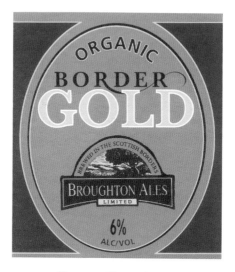

BORDER GOLD (6.0%)

Light-coloured, aromatic, organic ale, made using organic pale ale malt and New Zealand Hallertau hops. Available bottled and, occasionally, as a 'special' on draught. Should be served chilled.

BROUGHTON BEST (3.8%)

The brewery's only keg beer, Best is an extremely drinkable session ale.

CLIPPER'S IPA (4.2%)

Light-coloured, typical modern IPA in style, with a delicate aroma. Heavily hopped for a Broughton beer. Available on draught.

80/- ALE (4.2%)

Well-rounded, very malty draught ale, with hints of toffee and quite prominent hoppiness.

THE GHILLIE (4.5%)

Full-bodied, hoppy, malty ale, with hops most prominent in the finish and a spicy aroma. A 'ghillie' is a Scottish sporting attendant, and is particularly associated with game-fishing and stalking. The ghillie supplies the sportsman with physical assistance and local knowledge. Available in draught and bottled formats.

GREENMANTLE ALE (3.9%)

The first beer to be brewed by Broughton, it takes its name from the 1920 novel Greenmantle, *written by John Buchan, who spent much of his childhood in the area. Pale malt and roasted barley are blended in the production of Greenmantle, which is mid-brown in colour, hoppy and fruity. 'Bitter-sweet', according to the brewers. Available in draught and bottled formats.*

MERLIN'S ALE (4.2%)

Deep-golden in colour. Well-hopped, but the hops are balanced by fruit and malt flavours. Merlin reputedly lived near Broughton, and is said to be buried by a thorn bush which still stands on the banks of the River Tweed at Drumelzier. Nearby Stobo Kirk features a stained glass window that portrays St Mungo baptising Merlin in the Tweed. Available in cask and bottled formats.

OLD JOCK ALE (6.7%)

Strong and robust dark winter ale, quite sweet, spicy and fruity, with a powerful finish. An ideal accompaniment to strong meat or game. Some drinkers favour a 50/50 mix of Old Jock and Greenmantle Ale. Available in cask and bottled formats.

SCOTTISH OATMEAL STOUT (4.2%)

Very dry stout, made using roasted barley, pale malt, black malt, oatmeal and Goldings and Fuggles hops. The oatmeal gives it a slightly sweet and creamy taste, and the finish is quite fruity. 'Refreshing and nourishing', according to its brewers. Available in cask and bottled formats, with the label/pump clip featuring a portrait of the brewer Robert Younger (1820-1901), great-grandfather of Broughton's co-founder, David Younger.

CALEDONIAN

Caledonian Brewing Company Ltd, 42 Slateford Road,
Edinburgh EH11 1PH
www.caledonian-brewery.co.uk

tel: 0131 3371286 *fax*: 0131 3132370 *email*: info@caledonian-brewery.co.uk

The Caledonian Brewery is situated in Slateford Road and dates from 1869. It was founded by George Lorimer (1846-1939) and Robert Clark, Head Brewer at the Boroughloch Brewery. Lorimer was just 18 years old when he met Clark in 1865, soon after returning to Edinburgh from his job as a London tea-broker. He had gone back to his native city in order to assist his widowed mother after his father had been killed in the fire that destroyed Edinburgh's Theatre Royal in January 1865. Lorimer and Clark acquired land on the western outskirts of the city, and built an impressive, four-storey, red-brick brewery, which fronted the main Edinburgh-Lanark road. The brewery had its own wells, maltings, cooperage, and railway sidings. At the time of its construction, there were more than 40 operational breweries in Edinburgh. (See Heritage section.)

The company traded as Lorimer & Clark, producing Lorimer's Scotch Ale in cask, and bottled Merman India Pale Ale, along with Imperial Stout, Brown Stout and Double Brown Stout.

Robert Clark died of a chill at the age of 40 in 1874, but George Lorimer continued to run the business alone, until his retirement in 1919. By this time, the company had extensive markets in England, as well as throughout Scotland, and it was purchased by Vaux of Sunderland. Vaux wanted the Caledonian Brewery because of its reputation for making Scotch Ale in particular, there being a large market for the style in the north-east of England. Vaux purchased the business for the sum of £33,746. 6s. 8d, and most of the beer subsequently produced was sold south of the border.

During the next six decades, the brewery suffered from lack of investment, partly because physical expansion of the site was impossible. The cooperage and maltings were closed by the time the brewery's centenary was celebrated in 1969, but it did escape the drastic round of closures that decimated the industry during the 1960s.

By the mid-1980s, however, the Caledonian was surplus to Vaux's requirements and was closed in 1985, despite turning out some 1,600 barrels of beer per week prior to closure. This could well have been the end of one of the last of Edinburgh's breweries, but in 1987 Head Brewer Russell Sharp, formerly chief chemist for whisky company Chivas Bros, headed a management buy-out along with former Lorimer & Clark Managing Director Dan Kane, and the Caledonian Brewing Company Ltd was created.

A positive aspect of Vaux's lack of investment and upgrading at 'the Caley', as the brewery is popularly known in Edinburgh, was that Sharp and his team took possession of a truly traditional brewery, complete with direct-fired coppers—now the last such working coppers in Britain. Sharp claims that the use of the direct-fired coppers means that the wort and hops are correctly boiled, rather than 'stewed', which can be the result of steam-heating in stainless steel vessels. The brewery uses the marketing slogan 'Great beers brewed with real fire'.

A much less desirable 'real fire' in 1994 destroyed the maltings, but halted production for only a very short time, though reconstruction work took two years and £3m to complete. Even the brewery's yeast was damaged by the blaze, and new supplies to the original specification were obtained from the National Yeast Bank, where all brewers deposit samples of their yeast for just such a contingency.

A second fire in October 1998 destroyed one of the three original coppers, dating from 1869, but an identical replacement was hand-made by McMillan's of Prestonpans to the original plans, which were still in their possession. As much of the original copper as could be salvaged was incorporated into the new vessel.

Ironically, Vaux of Sunderland ceased trading in 1999, and the now-thriving Caledonian Brewing Company bought back the Lorimer & Clark brand name, subsequently producing Lorimer & Clark's India Pale Ale (5.3%). There are plans to reintroduce Lorimer's Scotch Ale, brewed in the traditional style that prevailed before production was transferred by Vaux to its Sunderland brewery.

By 1998 a new yeast room and cask-racking system had been created at the Caley, and in that year new settling tanks for keg beers were installed in a dedicated building. A kegging plant was assembled in a converted former barley store in order to produce the range of Calder's keg beers under contract for **Carlsberg-Tetley**, who closed their Alloa Brewery in the same year.

Having fought off a number of other contenders for the lucrative Calder's contract, Caledonian invested in excess of £2m in the new venture, which has the capacity to produce 50,000 barrels per year. According to Russell Sharp, 'I went to school in Alloa, and at that time there were still several breweries working there. When we got the chance to take over brewing Calder's, to keep the operation in Scotland, it seemed to me appropriate that we should do so. I'm very pleased that we are doing it, and we were able to take on two or three ex-Alloa Brewery staff as well.'

In addition to the 50,000 barrels of keg Calder's products being brewed each year, the Caledonian Brewery turns out a further 40,000 barrels per annum of cask, keg and bottled ales under its own name, some 80% of which is sold in cask format. Russell Sharp says that if pushed to its limits, the entire brewery could produce 120,000 barrels per year.

The Caledonian Brewery does not undertake any bottling or canning on the premises, and all beer destined for bottled sales is tankered south to Marston's in Burton upon Trent. Canning of Caledonian 80/- is carried out under contract by Scottish Courage.

'You can find casks of our beer from Land's End to John o' Groats,' claims Sharp, 'and even beyond that, as we have outlets on Orkney, and 80/- keg is sold on the St Ola ferry between Scrabster and Orkney.'

Carlsberg-Tetley act as distributors in Scotland, while Marston's distribute south of the border, and there are good markets for Caledonian ales in Yorkshire and the Midlands in particular. Keg beers are exported to France, the USA, Canada and Sweden.

Caledonian beers in bottled format are available in a wide range of supermarkets, including Asda, Safeway, Sainsbury's, Tesco and Waitrose, and the brewery produces an own-label organic lager for Tesco. Other outlets include Marks & Spencer stores, and off-licence chains such as Bottoms Up, Oddbins, and Victoria Wine.

In 1996 the Caledonian was the World Beer Guide's British Brewery of the Year. The beers themselves have been awarded many prizes, and those mentioned alongside the brands below are just a selection of the most recent and most prestigious.

Twelve 'specials' are brewed each year, some of which are seasonal 'regulars' while others are event-specific, one-off brews. In common with several other Scottish brewers, Caledonian produces a Burns Ale (4.7%) in January. The winter seasonal brew Double Amber (4.6%) is produced to an original recipe, and carries the name of Campbell, Hope & King, the well-regarded Edinburgh brewing company that was acquired by Whitbread and closed in 1970. (See Heritage section.) It is a full-bodied, mid-brown ale, fruity, with a hoppy finish. Murray's Pale Summer Ale (3.6%)is another regular seasonal beer, which commemorates the

Craigmillar brewing business of William Murray. (See Heritage section.) It is golden-coloured, quite bitter, but balanced by maltiness.

Tempus Fugit is the name given to bottle-conditioned versions of regular beers produced each year by the Caledonian. In 1997 Tempus Fugit was 80/-, in 1998 Deuchar's IPA, and in 1999 Golden Promise.

At the time of writing, there are plans to create a range of 'Caledonian Classics', which may include such beers as Campbell, Hope & King's Double Amber, Lorimer & Clark's 70/- and Merman XXX, along with a traditional stout.

Caledonian also produce 'house' ales for specific outlets, the most intriguing of which is Earthquake Ale, brewed exclusively for the Royal Hotel in Comrie, Perthshire. Comrie lies on the Highland Boundary Fault, and the ABV of the beer (4.5%) equates to the highest level of tremor registered in the area on the Richter Scale!

The Caledonian Brewery boasts an impressive visitor centre in the former maltings, managed by Ron Davies. There are conducted tours of the brewery at 11.00 am, 12.30 pm and 2.30 pm, Monday to Friday. Pre-booking is advisable, and group rates are available. Beer tasting in the attractive Sample Cellar concludes each tour, and is included in the admission price. The visitor centre hotline is 0131 6238066.

In addition to its visitor centre, the Caledonian Brewery also boasts a flexible events venue in the shape of the Festival Hall, formerly a barley store and later a bottling hall. The Hall hosts regular ceilidhs, and can be booked for parties, receptions, conferences and other gatherings, with a range of catering and entertainment packages available. Contact the hotline number for further information, or see the Caledonian website.

The brewery shop sells beer in bottles and cans, along with a range of branded merchandise, and purchases may also be made by mail order or online.

DEUCHAR'S INDIA PALE ALE (3.8%)

Deuchar's IPA revives an old-established Edinburgh brewing name and Pale Ale pioneer. (See Heritage section.) Deliciously thirst-quenching, smooth-bodied, quite peppery and tart in the mouth, and with a long hoppy finish—a classic of the genre. 1996 CAMRA Champion Beer of Scotland, and 2nd in Scottish Beer of the Year competition. Silver award in Bitter category at the Great British Beer Festival, London. 1998 Champion Beer of Scotland, and overall winner in Champion Beer of Scotland competition. 1999 bronze award in the overall championship of the 1999 Great British Beer Festival, and a silver award in the Bitter category. Again, a CAMRA Beer of the Year in 2000. The first Scottish beer to win at the Great British Beer Festival.

EDINBURGH STRONG ALE (6.4%)

Complex and distinctive, not overly sweet, unlike many other strong ales. Full-bodied, firm and smooth. Produced in draught format, though quite difficult to find, but commonly available bottled.

80/- (4.1%)

Malty, hoppy, smooth and nicely-balanced. Quite fruity, with a suggestion of chocolate from the chocolate malt used. 1996 and 1997 CAMRA Champion Beer of Scotland and Champion Beer at Scottish Beer of the Year competition. 1998 Champion Beer of Scotland, runner-up in Scottish Beer of the Year competition. A CAMRA Beer of the Year in 1999. Available in cask, keg, bottled and canned formats. The official beer of the 2000 Edinburgh International Festival.

FLYING SCOTSMAN (5.1%)

Dark ale with notes of bitter chocolate and almonds. Quite a dry, hoppy finish. Available in bottled format.

GOLDEN PROMISE (4.4%, bottled at 5%)

The world's first totally organic beer. Single variety organic Kent hops grown by Peter Hall are used, along with organically produced malted Scottish barley. Golden Promise takes its name from a variety of malting barley, though, ironically, Chariot barley is now used for this beer, while Golden Promise is utilised for all of the Caledonian's other beers. The organic version of Golden Promise simply does not produce a sufficiently high yield to make it viable for the Caledonian's purposes. Pale in colour, a nicely balanced, fragrant, malty beer with a floral, hoppy finish. Winner of the 1996 and 1997 Soil Association Organic Foods Awards-winner. Available in cask, and also bottled. The bottled version is marketed at the brew's original strength of 5.0%, while the hoppier draught version has been reduced in strength to 4.4%.

LORIMER & CLARK'S INDIA PALE ALE (5.3%)

A classic, hoppy IPA, available on draught in limited outlets.

MERMAN XXX (4.8%)

Rich, fruity, full-bodied and comparatively sweet, but in common with most Caledonian beers, it has a developing complexity. Brewed to an original Victorian recipe, Merman revives the name of one of Lorimer & Clark's original brands. Available in cask format only.

PORTER (4.1%)

Dark-coloured, dry, malty porter. Available in cask, usually just during the winter months.

CARLSBERG-TETLEY

Carlsberg-Tetley Scotland Ltd, Stuart House, Esk Mills Park,
Musselburgh EH21 7PB
www.carlsbergtetley.co.uk
tel*: 0131 665 3934* ***fax****: 0131 665 8719*

Carlsberg-Tetley is a wholly owned subsidiary of the Copenhagen-based Carlsberg company, and has operated since 1992, when Allied Breweries joined forces with the Danish lager brewing giant. The company has breweries in Leeds (the famous Joshua Tetley Brewery), and Northampton.

Until 1998 Carlsberg-Tetley had a Scottish brewing presence in the shape of Carlsberg-Tetley Alloa Ltd, which latterly produced Skol, Carlsberg, Castlemaine XXXX lagers and a range of ales under the name of Calder's. These commemorated the Alloa brewer John Calder, 'the Grand Old Man of Brewing', who spent 76 years working in the industry. (See Heritage section.) However, despite recent expenditure in the region of £2.5m, rationalisation brought about the closure of the Alloa plant, along with Carlsberg-Tetley breweries in Wrexham and Burton upon Trent.

Today, six keg Calder's products are brewed by the **Caledonian** Brewery, while canned Calder's Premium Cream Beer is brewed and packaged in Leeds. All of the lagers previously produced in Alloa now come out of the Northampton brewery.

Carlsberg-Tetley's Scottish operation was formerly administered from offices and a distribution depot located at the site of the now-demolished Drybrough's brewery in Craigmillar, Edinburgh, but the adminstration office was relocated to Musselburgh in February 2001. The Alloa Brewery site continues to be used as a distribution centre, and is home to the company's technical services and telesales departments.

Carlsberg-Tetley Scotland's Calder's products are the official beers of Scottish Rugby and the Scottish Rugby Union. Calder's beers are also the official ales of Gala RFC, Currie RFC, Stirling County RFC, Edinburgh Accies FC and Hawick RFC, and the company is club sponsor of Melrose RFC.

CALDER'S 80/- (4.2%)
Smooth, full-bodied, fruity keg ale.

CALDER'S EXPORT (4.2%)
Richly flavoured ale with roast malt aroma and taste.

CALDER'S LIGHT (2.8%)
Well-balanced, dark-coloured '60/-' ale.

CALDER'S PREMIUM CREAM BEER (4.5%)
Smooth, strong beer, the second-biggest seller in the premium 'nitrokeg' ale market in terms of volume and throughput.

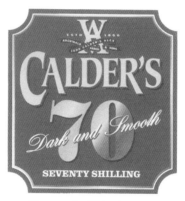

CALDER'S 70/- (3.6%)
Smooth, dark beer, quite full-bodied, and with roasted malt aroma and flavour.

CALDER'S SPECIAL (3.6%)
Smooth, full-bodied session beer with pronounced hoppy bitterness and fruit flavours.

CLOCKWORK

R. H. & J. G. Graham, the Clockwork Beer Company,
1153/55 Cathcart Road, Glasgow G42 9HB
tel: *0141 6490184* **fax**: *0141 6490643* **email**: *rhg@talk21.com*

Husband and wife team Robin and Gay Graham purchased a large, run-down, 1930s art deco-style pub, close to Scotland's Hampden national football stadium, and proceeded to renovate it during 1997.

Robin Graham says of the end result, 'I think we are fairly unusual in that a family can come into our premises—where we have a large no-smoking family area—and sample our ales without having to buy a meal. We serve bar snacks and meals all day, but one does not have to eat to indulge.'

The Grahams added a five-barrel micro-brewery to their operation, and this is visible through a glass window in the bar area. It produces between 1,200 and 1,400 pints per brew. Brewing began in December 1997, with American hops featuring in most of the beers, which tend to be quite light and bitter in character, and are unfiltered.

'We only brew for our pub, and we know the clientele and what they like,' explains Robin Graham, who is not, however, afraid to be experimental when it comes to new products and 'specials'. The Clockwork is also innovative in that it must be the only brewery in the country that disposes of its waste barley via an ostrich farm, where it provides a nutritious feed for the birds!

'We're a hoppy pub,' says Robin, and, indeed, his operation is part of the trend in Scottish brew-pubs to turn around the old idea that beers for the Scottish palate have to be sweet and comparatively lightly hopped. The Grahams also boast that their pub offers one of the largest selections of Belgian and German beers in Britain.

A range of fruit beers is produced under the name 'Hazy Daze', a title which reflects the fact that if you use real fruit in the recipe, the beer can never be truly clear. According to Robin Graham, drinkers complain if they don't get a cloudy pint! The Hazy Daze range is produced by taking the brewery's 'lagered' beers as a base, and fermenting them for a second time using fresh fruit and spices. Robin Graham notes that 'each keg can use up to 20 pounds of fresh fruit', and the collection has included banana, kiwi and raspberry, while Seriously Ginger is a perennial favourite. Fruit beers are produced as and when the raw material is available.

Additionally, a monthly special (at 4.1%) is brewed, using European—usually English—hops for drinkers who prefer that style of beer, and the Clockwork's specials are now significant sellers. 'We also take off some "uncut" ale and create a strong version of the specials, usually at 6.0% ABV,' says Robin.

One of Robin Graham's more idiosyncratic specials during late 2000 was Original Kelpie, a dark, 4.1% beer, which was an attempt to reproduce the style of ale made on the Scottish islands in days gone by. Along with Bruce Williams, Robin Graham was the originator of Kelpie Organic Seaweed Ale (see **Heather**), and with Original Kelpie Robin went one stage further, using not just seaweed but also peat in the mashing process. 'The ultimate island beer,' he reckons.

Brewery tours may be arranged.

AMBER IPA (3.8%)

A light IPA with a North American flowery hop style, brewed using Oregon 'Liberty' hops in the boil for flavour, and 'finished' with Cascade hops for aroma. Amber IPA has citrus notes on the nose, a malty flavour, and a crisp, hoppy finish. A strong version at 5.5% is sometimes brewed under the name Oregon IPA.

KEY WEISSE BIER (5.0%)

Robin Graham describes Key Weisse as 'our version of a fresh white beer, usually made in the southern areas of Germany, and Bavaria in particular. Produced from a half wheat malt, a blend of lager malt and organic wheat flour, while being flavoured with generous German hops. A genuine German yeast culture is used.' Key Weisse has an aroma of citrus fruit, a sour bread flavour, and a well-balanced, bitter-sweet finish. It is cloudy in the best traditions of the genre, due to the fact that the yeast is retained in the final product. A very dry, Raspberry Weisse Bier (at 5.0%) is also permanently available.

ORIGINAL LAGER (4.8%)

Brewed to the principles of the famous sixteenth-century Rhinehiestsgabot or German Purity Law, Original Lager incorporates lager malt, German hops, yeast and water. It is cold-fermented and cold-conditioned for at least six weeks before being served, and is dispensed under a low level of carbonation. The result is a lager with a soft malt texture, rich, dry flavour and a clean, malty finish. Robin Graham notes that 'when we use any unusual hops we can create a strong "real ale" version of the lager, usually at 6.0% ABV. The name we give it varies according to the time of year.'

RED ALT BEER (4.4%)

According to Robin, 'this unique fusion between two styles of beer is born from the original German alt beer crossed with an American red ale.' Red Alt has a fruity and malty aroma, a caramel-like flavour, and an emphatic flowery, hoppy finish. A 6.0% strong version of Red Alt is sometimes brewed under the name Thunder & Lightning.

DEVON

Devon Ales Ltd, 7 Main Street, Sauchie,
Alloa FK10 3JR
tel: *01259 722020 fax: 01259 781324* **email***: john.gibson@btinternet.com*

Pub-brewery attached to the Mansfield Arms in the Clackmannanshire village of Sauchie. According to publican and brewer John Gibson, 'The brewery takes its name from the local Devon mine. It's a pub brewery, catering for the tastes of our customers, quite a few of whom are ex-miners. So what we brew are miners' ales in style.'

John Gibson has been based at the Mansfield Arms for sixteen years, and has been making beer there for the last nine. 'I learnt to brew by trial and error and by buying a book,' he says. He operates a five-barrel brewhouse, producing an average of twelve barrels per week. With the exception of the occasional cask that finds its way to a beer festival, all the beer brewed by Devon Ales is sold in the Mansfield Arms and John's second pub, the nearby Inn at Muckhart. 'There are just four ingredients in all our beers,' he says, 'water, hops, malt and yeast. We could be brewing in Bavaria.'

Three regular cask beers are on offer, and 'specials' are produced from time to time. In the past, the range of specials has included a cask-conditioned lager.

Brewery tours may be arranged.

ORIGINAL (3.8%)
A good session ale, malty, with a sprinkling of Styrian hops.

PRIDE (4.9%)
Strong, malty, quite hoppy beer. 'A connoisseur's ale,' says John Gibson.

THICK BLACK (4.1%)
A characterful Scottish stout. 'There's a brewery in Dublin trying to copy it,' reckons Gibson, 'but I doubt stout will ever catch on in Ireland!'

EGLESBRECH ALE
HOUSE

Eglesbrech Ale House, 14 Melville Street, Falkirk FH1 1HZ
www.behindthewall.co.uk
tel: *01324 633338* ***fax***: *01324 613258*

The Eglesbrech Ale House occupies the upstairs of the Behind the Wall restaurant/café/bar complex, which opened in Falkirk in 1985. The building dates from the 1920s, and was originally a Playtex bra factory, which gives a whole new meaning to the idea of a drinker being 'in his cups'!

'Eglesbrech' is derived from the Gaelic for 'speckled kirk', and is an old name for what later became Falkirk. The brewery building occupies the site of a former cinema, where during the Second World War, Haddow's reputedly blended Eglesbrech whisky, a bottle of which is displayed in the bar.

The brewery opened in September 2000 after a number of test brews had been carried out at Bruce Williams' Craigmill brewery at Strathaven, and the heather ale maestro remains an influential figure in the Eglesbrech project. Scott Robertson and Alan Falconer carry out the actual brewing.

With the opening of the Eglesbrech, brewing has returned to Falkirk for the first time since the acquisition of James Aitken's substantial brewing business by Northern Breweries in 1960. Aitken's had been founded in 1740, and became one of the 'lost' breweries of Scotland in the mid-1960s. (See Heritage section.)

Beer is produced in a five-barrel brew plant, which is currently worked once a week, and some is supplied to two other outlets in the same ownership as Behind the Wall. There are tentative plans to bottle beers at the **Forth** Brewery and to create a visitor centre, with a tasting area and merchandise for sale.

ALT BEER (4.4%)
A red-coloured, strongly flavoured beer, with a complex blend of malt and hops. Available seasonally.

ANTONINE ALE (3.9%)
A traditional 70/- ale, dark coloured, with a soft, subtle malt aroma and a light texture. Not heavily hopped, and comparatively sweet. Named after the Antonine Wall, which ran through the centre of what is now the town of Falkirk, and was built between the Forth and Clyde by the Romans in 140-42AD to defend their northernmost position in Britain. Antonine Ale was the second Eglesbrech beer to be launched, and was christened after a local newspaper appeal for a suitable name. It is available as a 'seasonal' brew.

EAGLE'S BREATH (4.1%)
Very dry, bitter beer, available on an occasional basis.

FALKIRK 400 (3.8%)
A blonde, straw-coloured ale, with a spicy aroma. It has a light malt texture and very dry flavour, with a hoppy, dry finish. Of the IPA genre, but with the addition of ginger, bog-myrtle and dandelions! This was the first beer brewed by Eglesbrech, and it takes its name from the fact that 2000 was the 400th anniversary of Falkirk's burgh charter, granted by King James VI.

TALL BLONDE (4.0%)
Quite malty and characterful Czech-style session lager, which has proved very popular with the Eglesbrech drinkers.

FAR NORTH

Far North Brewery, Melvich Hotel, Melvich, Sutherland KW14 7YJ
tel*: 01641 531206* ***fax****: 01641 531347* ***email****: melvichtl@aol.com*

The Far North Brewery is attached to the Melvich Hotel on the north coast of Sutherland. It is the northernmost mainland brewing operation in Britain, and is run by Borders-born former accountant-turned-hotelier Peter Martin. Peter had been a 'hobby brewer' for some 20 years while working in London, prior to returning to his native country and acquiring the Melvich Hotel four years ago.

On 1 July 2000 the first Far North beer was brewed, and Peter currently turns out just a firkin (72 pints) per week, principally to meet the demands of his paying guests, as the locals have still not fully embraced the concept of 'real ale'. Many of his guests are English, and stay at the Melvich Hotel while working at the nearby Dounreay nuclear installation.

Peter hopes to have a five-barrel brewhouse in operation in the near future, at which point he plans to spread the cask ale gospel by trying to get his beers into some other outlets across the Highlands. He reports that there is already considerable interest in his brewing activities from people on the 'beer trail', who call in at Melvich after visiting the **Isle of Skye** Brewery, and before catching the ferry from nearby Scrabster to visit **Orkney** and its brewery at Quoyloo.

EDGE OF DARKNESS (approx 7.0%)
Seasonal winter ale, strong and dark, not unlike Theakston's Old Peculier in character. Brewed using a blend of pale, crystal, chocolate and black malt. 'Edge of Darkness' was a 1986 TV political thriller, with the action focusing on a nuclear waste plant, hence the name for this beer, drunk principally by Dounreay staff!

PFR (4.8%)
The name of this strong, characterful and hoppy ale is also designed to please Peter Martin's Dounreay devotees. PFR stands for Prototype Fast Reactor!

REAL MACKAY (3.8%)
The Far North's regular ale, Real Mackay is more heavily hopped and bitter than many traditional Scottish beers. Full-bodied, and in character seems stronger than its ABV would suggest. Brewed using pale and crystal malts, and late-hopped with Styrian Goldings.

FISHERROW

Fisherrow Brewery Ltd, Unit 12, Duddingston Yards,
Duddingston Park South, Edinburgh EH15 3NX
www.fisherrow.co.uk
***tel**: 0131 6215501 **fax**: 0131 6219552 **email**: sales@fisherrow.co.uk*

Fisherrow Brewery opened in November 1999, and is situated in a pair of modern industrial units in the Craigmillar area of Edinburgh. Craigmillar was once a popular location for breweries, and the development of Fisherrow revives brewing tradition in the district, which was lost with the closure of Drybrough's Brewery. (See Heritage section.) The brewery takes its name from Whitelaw's Fisherrow Brewery, which operated in nearby Musselburgh, and was a casualty of Whitbread rationalisation during the 1960s. In its heyday, there were five breweries in the Fisherrow district.

Of the dozens of breweries that once graced Edinburgh, only four currently operate, with the vast **Scottish Courage** Fountain Brewery and the **Caledonian** being the largest and longest-established, while **McCowan's** and Fisherrow make up the quartet. The city's Rose Street Brewery, Beer Necessities, and the Physician & Firkin brew-pub all closed during 1999, and Iain Turnbull of Fisherrow proclaims that theirs is 'the third-largest brewery in Edinburgh!'

Chief Executive of Fisherrow is David Murray, while Iain Turnbull is Head Brewer and Assistant Brewer is Karen Hetherington. David has a postgraduate diploma in Brewing and Distilling from Heriot-Watt University and, like Iain, is a former Courage employee. All three were previously involved in Edinburgh's Restalrig Village Brewery, which opened in the former Munrospun building in late 1997 and closed less than two years later, having produced more than twenty different brews during its short life. In addition to her brewing duties, Karen produces designs for pump clips and is responsible for Fisherrow's logo, stationery, website and sales material.

Fisherrow was the first brewery—in Britain, at any rate—to record its creation on the internet, with regularly posted pictures of work in progress. The brew-plant is somewhat idiosyncratic, featuring a number of pieces of former dairy equipment. Iain Turnbull says that the brewing copper 'came off the back of a lorry', which is true, since it was formerly a lorry-mounted milk tanker!

The fermentation vessels were previously Tennent's cellar tanks, and have a total capacity of 40 barrels, though it is anticipated that this will be expanded to 60 barrels before long. The brew-plant has a maximum capacity of 13 barrels, and an average of 25 barrels are produced each week.

Fisherrow concentrates on brewing traditional-style cask real ales. It has six beers in its 'Regular' range and offers on a request basis a further five in its 'Scottish' range. The brewers note that 'traditional Scottish beers are sweeter and less well-hopped than popular English styles'. In addition to these eleven beers, a dozen 'specials' were also produced during Fisherrow's first year in operation, and the plan is to brew a quarterly special in addition to modest quantities of two monthly specials. Like Douglas Ross of **Bridge of Allan** Brewery, Fisherrow produced a beer to celebrate Euro 2000. They played it safe, however, by brewing Howzat (4.0%) for the cricket version of the competition—for which Scotland did qualify!

Around 95% of the brewery's beer is delivered directly, keeping Fisherrow's three employees in close contact with customers, and ensuring that casks are fresh when delivered to points of sale. Scottish markets tend to be concentrated in the Central Belt and as far north as Aberdeen, while a trading arrangement with **Heather Ale Ltd** gets Fisherrow beers into bars on the west coast.

South of the border, there are strong markets on Tyneside and in Yorkshire, as well as in the north-west and Wales, while Birmingham and the London area also sell significant quantities of Fisherrow products. A number of agents and wholesalers do cover specific areas of the country, but Iain Turnbull says: 'Just ring the brewery if you want something. If you don't see what you want in our existing range, ask us and we'll try to brew it for you.'

Projects for the future include producing a range of branded merchandise, and bottling some Fisherrow beers, probably in bottle-conditioned format. Own-label bottling for customers would almost certainly follow on from such a venture.

In addition to their own brewing business, the Fisherrow team also designs and builds breweries for other companies, with one such venture being the creation of the Malvern Hills Brewery in Worcestershire.

Brewery visits by arrangement.

Regular Range:

BURGH BITTER (4.2%)
Thirst-quenching, pale golden bitter, quite full-bodied and hoppy, yet slightly sweet. Described as the brewery's 'flagship ale'.

EXPORT PALE ALE (5.2%)
Pale in colour, with a distinctive hoppy and fruity character, attributed by the brewers to the inclusion of Slovenian and American hops. Refreshing and deceptively drinkable.

HOPPING MAD (4.2%)
Pale golden ale with distinctive fruity aroma and taste, and hints of vanilla. First brewed as a 'special' in March 2000, but now, due to its popularity, part of the regular range. Described by its brewers as a 'quaffable spring ale'.

INDIA PALE ALE (3.8%)
A complex blend of hops makes this refreshing in the best traditions of the style. Deceptively full-bodied for its strength, an ideal session ale.

NUT BROWN ALE (4.8%)
Dark red in colour, this is a traditional brown ale, more usually found in bottles than on draught. Full malt flavour, warming.

PORTOBELLO PORTER (4.5%)
Based on a nineteenth-century recipe from Robert Black's Devanha Brewery in Aberdeen, this porter was originally produced as a 'special', but proved sufficiently popular to be added to the regular range during 2000. 'Draught tarmac' is Iain Turnbull's initial description, before he provides a more specific assessment, relating to the wide range of different malts in the recipe, which includes an element of peated malt. Very black in colour, dry, smooth and complex, with the creamy-brown head tradition- ally associated with the genre.

Scottish Range:

80/- (4.4%)
A traditional, dark-coloured Scottish session beer.

GOLDEN HEAVY (4.0%)
A pale-gold heavy beer, malty, with a subtle hoppy aftertaste. The recipe is based on the sort of traditional Scottish heavies that would have been a staple of the old Fisherrow area breweries.

LEITH DARK HEAVY (4.8%)
Traditional brown heavy, with full malt flavour and quite strong hop aroma and taste.

70/- (4.1%)
Mid-brown session beer, quite sweet, complex, with a lightly hoppy finish.

60/- (3.8%)
Similar in character to the India Pale Ale (above), but slightly sweeter and darker.

FORTH

Forth Brewery Company Ltd, Eglinton, Kelliebank, Alloa FK10 1NU
www.forthbrewery.com
tel: *01259 725511* ***fax***: *01259 725522*
email:*duncankellock@forthbrewery.freeserve.co.uk*

The Forth Brewery was established on a site close to the River Forth on the outskirts of the famous old brewing town of Alloa in the summer of 1999. Chief Executive and Head Brewer at Forth is Duncan Kellock, who spent 20 years with Alloa's **Maclay** company, having previously worked for Vaux at their St Leonard's Brewery, until that ceased production in 1977. For the last seven years, Duncan was Head Brewer for the Maclay Group, and the development of the new brewery came about when Maclay's decided to stop brewing on their Thistle Brewery site in the centre of Alloa.

The Forth is jointly owned by the Maclay Group, Duncan Kellock, Heather Ale Ltd, John Sinclair Haulage and three private investors, all of whom have equal shares.

The new brewery is aptly housed in buildings that date from 1884, and were part of George Younger's export bottling plant. (See Heritage section.) Most of the bottling complex was burnt down in 1961, but the site was owned by John Sinclair Haulage and was ideal for the new operation.

The Forth Brewery name is not a new one, as John Knox & Son operated a brewery at Cambus, near Alloa, for nearly a century from the 1860s, which traded as the Forth for most of its existence. In 1957 it was sold and subsequently developed into a whisky distillery (See Heritage section.)

The principles behind the creation of the 'new' Forth Brewery were to develop a modern, flexible, cost-effective brewing, bottling and packaging facility, which could produce its own range of draught and bottled beers and lagers and also undertake contract-brewing and bottling for other Scottish brewers.

The Forth is a 40-barrel operation, which turns out some 9,000 barrels per year, making it the fifth-largest brewery in Scotland. So, despite its relative youth and comparative obscurity, the Forth is by no means a minor-league player in the Scottish brewing industry. The bottling line can handle 3,500 bottles per hour, and is the fourth biggest in the country. Four of the nine staff employed at Forth were formerly with Maclay's, while others have experience from Carlsberg-Tetley's Alloa Brewery. Some of the brewing equipment was purchased second-hand from Maclay's and from the Alloa Brewery, so there is an element of physical continuity in Alloa's beer-making heritage. The bottling plant is, however, new and of Italian origin.

In addition to their own range of products, a major part of Forth's business consists of brewing for Maclay's on a contract basis. Three keg beers, are produced, namely Coopers, Stirling and Thistle. Alba, Ebulum, Fraoch, Grozet and Kelpie are brewed and bottled for Heather Ale Ltd, while Independence Lager is produced for the Scottish National Party, and St Johnstone FC Lager for the Perth Premier League football club. Contract-brewing is also undertaken for a number of well-known, smaller Scottish brewing companies.

Forth Brewery products are available on draught in a range of Central Scotland outlets, and in bottled format through Maclay's and a variety of independent sources. Beers Scotland Limited (www.beers-scotland.co.uk) also represent Forth, along with a number of other small breweries. Puffer Ale and Saaz Organic Lager are available in some Safeway stores, and Duncan Kellock says 'bottled beer sales in supermarkets is the future for the Forth Brewing company'.

Duncan anticipates having visitor facilities at the Forth Brewery in place during 2001. Guided tours will be available, with the opportunity to purchase the firm's products in a retail establishment at the rear of the premises.

BANNOCKBURN (5.9%)
Traditional Scotch ale aimed principally at the US market, and strictly for export sales only. Bottled and sold in four-packs as 'Battlefield Beer'.

PUFFER ALE (4.1%)
More hoppy than its stablemate, Steamboat, Puffer is a tasty, characterful ale, with a peppery note, thanks to the use of Fuggles hops. Available in cask and bottled.

STEAMBOAT ALE (4.0%)
The first cask-conditioned ale to be brewed by Forth, with production commencing in February 2000. Steamboat is golden in colour, with a strong, malty character, courtesy of Maris Otter malt. Available in cask.

SAAZ (4.2%)
Organic lager with surprising complexity, cold-filtered to produce a cleaner, fresher flavour. A nice marriage of Scots organic lager malt and continental Hallertau Tradition hops. Produced since May 2000 and available bottled.

FYFE

Fyfe Brewing Company, 469 High Street,
Kirkcaldy, Fife KY1 2SN
www.fyfebrew.pwp.blueyonder.co.uk
tel/fax: *01592 646211* ***email:*** *fyfebrew@cableinet.co.uk*

The Fyfe Brewing Company was founded in 1995 by former accountant Nick Bromfield and his wife Gillie in a converted sail works located behind their popular Kirkcaldy pub, the Harbour Bar, where they have been based for the past nine years. The Harbour Bar was voted Kingdom of Fife CAMRA 'pub of the year' in 1999 and 2000.

As a range of industries developed in Fife during the eighteenth and nineteenth centuries, breweries were founded to slake the thirst of the workers in the coastal towns on the north shore of the Forth. By the 1820s there were five breweries in Kirkcaldy alone, with more than 20 operating in the county by the middle of the century. Fife was a good centre for brewing, as there were abundant supplies of barley available in the area, along with locally-mined coal to provide heat and power.

The only Fife brewery to survive beyond the First World War, however, was the Macduff Brewery in East Wemyss, near Kirkcaldy. Although brewing ceased in the late 1920s, following a takeover by the Edinburgh company of Murray & Co Ltd, the premises were used for bottling and distribution purposes for many years.

The Fyfe was the first brewery to be established in the county for more than 70 years and, for a time, it was one of three operating in quite close proximity. However, Backdykes at Thornton, near Kirkcaldy, closed during the early part of 2000, and Burntisland, to the west of Kirkcaldy on the Fife coast, has also now ceased trading.

Although he had considerable experience of the licenced trade, Nick Bromfield was a complete novice when he began brewing at the Harbour Bar, and called upon the services of brewing consultant Graham Moss to point him in the right direction. The brewery has a two-and-a-half-barrel plant, giving it a capacity of some 10 barrels per week. The Fyfe Brewing Company serves the Harbour Bar and a number of local outlets, while casks are also available via wholesalers, principally the two Yorkshire companies, the Flying Firkin and the Kitchen Brewery. Via these distributors, Fyfe ales have been known to find their way as far afield as the Isle of Wight.

Nick Bromfield regularly brews specials, including a blackcurrant-flavoured 7.3% ale called Widowmaker. He hopes that in a year or two the Fyfe Brewing Company can transfer into larger, less confined premises, where he does not have to carry every bag of malt up a flight of stairs into the brewhouse! If such a move does happen, then bottling of Fyfe ales for export is on the agenda.

Brewery tours are available by arrangement, and items of memorabilia, including Cauld Turkey T-shirts and brewery sweatshirts are also for sale.

AULD ALLIANCE (4.0 %)
Named in commemoration of the historic links between Scotland and France, Auld Alliance is a dark brown, fruity, hoppy ale with a long, dry aftertaste. A hefty dose of Target hops makes this, in the words of the brewers, 'a ferociously dry ale'.

CAULD TURKEY (6.0%)
Strong, full-bodied, fruity, ruby-coloured seasonal ale—appropriately brewed for Christmas.

FYFE FYRE (4.8%)
Straw-coloured, fruity, flavoursome ale, with a distinctly hoppy finish. The ale takes its name from the fact that in 1633 two local people convicted of witchcraft were burnt at the stake on Kirkcaldy shore.

LION SLAYER (4.2%)
Refreshing, dry ale, made using US Cascade hops. First brewed as a 'special' for the St Albans Beer Festival, where the name was chosen because the festival had a Roman theme. Lion Slayer was first marketed as Lion Shagger and is still sold as such in the Harbour Bar, but what Nick Bromfield describes as 'a degree of customer resistance' led to the tamer version of the name being used when the beer is on general sale.

ROPE OF SAND (3.7%)
Amber-coloured, dry, quite light-bodied IPA-style of beer. Brewed using the First Gold dwarf hop variety, which gives Rope of Sand its IPA identity. A thirst-quenching session bitter, it takes its name from the legend that Michael Scott—the Wizard of the North—was called upon by the people of Kirkcaldy to deal with the devil, who was causing them considerable trouble. Scott, who lived in a castle on the outskirts of the town, challenged the devil to plait a rope from sand. The devil was unable to do so and disappeared in a cloud of sulphurous fumes.

HARVIESTOUN

Harviestoun Brewery Ltd, Devon Road, Dollar,
Clackmannanshire FK14 7LX
tel: *01259 742141* ***fax***: *743141* ***email***: *harviestoun@talk21.com*

Harviestoun Brewery stands in the shadow of the Ochil Hills at Dollar, in Clackmannanshire, and is located in a 200-year-old former farm byre. The brewery was founded in 1984 by Ken Brooker and Eric Harris, using surplus brewing plant from a variety of sources, including copper boilers from the Alloa Brewery. Spurred on by the venture's initial success, a new, ten-barrel brew-plant was installed at Harviestoun five years later, having being acquired from the failed Devanha Brewery in Aberdeenshire.

Ken Brooker hails from Essex, and was a keen home-brewer who worked for the Ford Motor Company for 24 years before deciding to turn his hobby into a business, aided by his wife Ingrid, who acts as company secretary. Ken Brooker and Eric Harris now share brewing duties with former Vaux brewer Stewart Cail, and the beers they produce have won an enviable collection of awards over the years.

Ken Brooker sums up his personal views on brewing styles by saying 'I enjoy hops, my passion is the flavour from the hops. I like to make light-coloured beers so that the hop is the primary flavour.'

The brewery has a capacity of just over 100 barrels per week, but the average output is around 50 barrels. Some 70 Scottish outlets are supplied directly with cask ales, while 80% of cask sales are through wholesalers, which means that Harviestoun ales may be found on tap in bars the length and breadth of Britain. Small quantities of cask ale are also exported to the USA and Sweden.

Brooker's Bitter & Twisted and Schiehallion are contract-brewed for bottle format by **Belhaven**, who undertake all bottling work for Harviestoun. Bottled Harviestoun beers are to be found in a number of major supermarkets, with Schiehallion and Bitter & Twisted being available in Scottish branches of Safeway and Sainsbury, while Bitter & Twisted is now stocked by Safeway in England, too. Waitrose sells Liberation Ale, which is also on sale in Tesco, along with Old Engine Oil.

Many off-licences and specialist stores stock Harviestoun bottled beer, and the range is available online at www.beers-scotland.co.uk.

In addition to its regular draught and bottled beers, Harviestoun produces a dozen seasonal brews per year, some of which are perennial favourites, such as December's Good King Legless (4.5%) and the summer beer Belgian White (4.3%). Ken Brooker makes the point that his specials are all unique and created from scratch, and are not just 'adulterated versions of existing products', which is sometimes the case in other, larger breweries.

BROOKER'S BITTER & TWISTED (3.8%)

A very hoppy, blond beer with fruit flavours and a bitter finish. According to Ken Brooker it is 'bitter with a lemony twist to it. A nice, light, quaffing beer with a refreshing grapefruit and lemon flavour.' Champion Beer of Scotland 1999 and Bronze award winner in the Bitter category of the 2000 Great British Beer Festival. A runner-up in the 2000 Champion Beer of Scotland competition. First produced in 1997, available in cask, and since February 2000 also in bottle. Bitter & Twisted was named by Ingrid Brooker, who reckoned it was how her husband was feeling after losing his driving licence for speeding!

LIBERATION CHAMPION ALE (4.7%)

Strong hoppy character, refreshing and flowery, with a long aftertaste. Winner of the 'small brewers' category of the Tesco Beer Challenge 1999. The brewery's first venture into the bottled market.

OLD ENGINE OIL (6.0%)

The latest bottled brew from Harviestoun, Old Engine Oil is so named partly because of Ken Brooker's lengthy connection with the motor industry, and partly because of its colour and texture, though happily not its flavour! It is an extremely characterful beer, full-bodied, smooth and hoppy and with a distinctive flavour of treacle. Winner of the Winter 2000 Tesco Beer Challenge and available from Tesco stores in Scotland, where it is reported to have sold very well since its launch before Christmas 2000. Old Engine Oil will, in future, also make occasional appearances in draught format.

PTARMIGAN (4.5%)

Nicely-balanced cask beer with a good blend of hops, malt and fruit on the nose and palate. Bavarian Saaz hops are used for their particularly appealing bouquet, and Scottish Pale and Wheat malts predominate, hence Ptarmigan's blond colour. The beer was first introduced in 1992 and remains one of Harviestoun's most popular products.

SCHIEHALLION (4.8%)

Cask lager. Malty, hoppy, quite floral on the nose, and with a bitter finish. Winner of more Gold awards than any other Scottish cask product, including three at the Great British Beer Festival, the latest being in the Speciality Beer category in 1999. Schiehallion was also a CAMRA Beer of the Year (Speciality Beers category) in 2000. Brewed in the true continental fashion, using imported pale lager malt and Bavarian Hersbrucker hops. The lager is cold-fermented and stored for a lengthy period before consumption. It is served, unfiltered at cellar temperature. Named after a distinctive 3,500 ft mountain situated near Kinloch Rannoch in Perthshire. Available in cask and, since January 2000, also in bottled format.

TURNPIKE (4.1%)

A tawny, refreshingly bitter beer, brewed using Liberty and Willamette hops, the latter giving Turnpike its herbal and blackcurrant aroma.

WEE STOATER (3.6%)

Light in alcohol but strong in flavour, due to the use of East Kent Goldings and Styrian hops. Pale and crystal malts are used in the grist, along with wheat and oats. Wee Stoater takes its name from a West of Scotland expression that roughly translates as 'small cracker' and is frequently applied to women.

HEATHER

Heather Ale Ltd, Craigmill Brewery, Craigmill, Strathaven,
Lanarkshire ML10 6PB
www.heatherale.co.uk
tel: *01357 529529* ***fax***: *522256* ***email***: *fraoch@heatherale.co.uk*

Heather ale is an ancient drink (see Heritage section), and its modern recreation was the brainchild of Bruce Williams, who first produced it in 1992 at the now-defunct West Highland Brewery in Taynuilt. It was based on a sixteenth-century Gaelic recipe that had been discovered in the Hebrides, and was said to be ten generations old.

Bruce Williams's father set up the Glasgow Homebrew Shop during the 1960s, and the precious recipe was given to Bruce in the shop during 1986. His version of heather ale is marketed as Fraoch (pronounced fru-och). 'Leann fraoch' is Gaelic for heather ale. In 1993 brewing was transferred to **Maclay's** Thistle Brewery in Alloa, where the beer was made annually during the heather season in August and September. With the closure of the Thistle Brewery in 1999, production of the bottled range of Heather ales moved along the road to the new **Forth** Brewery. Heather Ale Ltd has a share in the Forth operation, and Bruce Williams's brother, Scott, acts as Managing Director.

Meanwhile Bruce had purchased Craigmill, a derelict 200-year-old former grain mill, situated on the River Avon, near Strathaven in Lanarkshire. The building was restored with the aid of Historic Scotland, and brewing of the cask versions of the Heather Ale range began in October 1999, utilising local spring water.

The brewery has a capacity of some 36 barrels per week, and output during 2000/2001 was running at around 1,000 barrels per annum. Some of the brewing plant came from Tennent's Wellpark establishment, and some is former dairy equipment. The stainless steel vessel, now clad in pinewood for the infusion of barley-malt and water, started life with dog biscuit manufacturer Spillers!

Casks of Heather Ale beers can be found in the south and west of England due to the efforts of wholesalers, as well as in quite a wide range of Scottish outlets. Bottled Heather Ale products are available in specialist beer stores, while Fraoch can be purchased from Scottish branches of Safeway and Sainsbury, with the latter also stocking Grozet. Around 80% of the ales brewed by Heather Ale Ltd are sold in bottled format.

The USA is an important export market for the Heather Ale range, with Mel Gibson flying 20 cases of Fraoch into Los Angeles in order to lubricate celebrations when his film *Braveheart* won an Oscar. The ale also sells well in Canada, France, Germany and Ireland.

Bruce and his brother Scott run Heather Ale Ltd, with Bruce describing his brother as 'the numerically literate one of us'. Both were previously involved in producing Glenbrew homebrew kits for the US market, which gave scope for the creation of a malty Scottish-style ale. They also made malt extract, and ran a winery in the slightly implausible setting of Clydebank.

Bruce Williams is a dynamic figure on the contemporary Scottish brewing scene, and he has even been dubbed 'the Woody Guthrie of the Scottish beer revival'! Bruce describes himself as 'just a beer and brewing enthusiast who can't help getting involved in new projects'.

He was responsible for helping Robin Graham establish his **Clockwork** Brewing Co. in Glasgow, and enjoyed a similar role with **Maclachlan's** brew-pub, for which he continues to act as a consultant. As well as his major, ongoing involvement with the Forth Brewery, Bruce has most recently played an important part in the creation and development of the **Eglesbrech** Ale House's brewing venture in Falkirk.

Heather Ale Ltd has gained a well-earned reputation for innovation, and for taking Scottish brewing back to its roots, experimenting with old recipes and reintroducing old styles of Scottish ales. Heather Ales' philosophy is: 'utilise indigenous resources and produce historic ales'. According to Bruce Williams, the difficulty of cultivating hops in Scotland meant that 'in olden times the Scots looked for any possible alternatives that were available in the different seasons of the year'. Eighteenth-century legislation made it illegal to brew ale using any principal ingredients other than malt and hops, and that legislation remains on the statute books. Every time Bruce Williams brews he risks a fine of £100 or three months in prison, but he reckons that the publicity generated by such an occurrence would be well worth the penalty!

In addition to the regular and recurring seasonal range of cask and bottled ales, as outlined below, Heather Ale also produces what they call 'Stone Kettle Specials'. The stone kettle is an attractive feature of the brewery, and is a 500-gallon stone-clad brewing vessel, built to an eighteenth-century design.

Specials produced between August 2000 and March 2001 included A. T. Bob (a slightly citrus-flavoured 80/- ale), and Swallow IPA. Significantly, Swallow was brewed using hops grown in the Clyde Valley, and was the first commercial beer to be produced with Scottish hops. The famous Duncan Macrae monologue 'The Wee Cock Sparra' gave its name to Cock Sparra, a red, malty ale with a dry finish, while January saw the brewing of Cask Stout, followed two months later by Bow Bakitt Bitter. The latter takes its name from a bridge over the River Avon, near Strathaven.

Visitors are welcome at Craigmill, though creation of a dedicated reception facility, exhibition area and shop in the basement of the mill is an ongoing project. Bottled beers and merchandise may be purchased online or on a mail-order basis.

ALBA (7.5%)

Scots pine ale. Strong, amber-coloured ale with an aroma of spruce. Malty, woody and faintly medicinal, with a long, attractive finish. Ales made from spruce and pine were introduced to Scotland by the Vikings, and continued to be brewed until the late nineteenth century, being particularly popular in Aberdeenshire. They were regularly taken on long sea voyages, as they helped to prevent outbreaks of scurvy. According to Bruce Williams, the spruce ale made on Shetland must have been very special, as it was said to 'stimulate animal instincts' and give women twins—presumbly not without a little assistance from a man, however impressive the beverage. Sprigs of pine are harvested in April and May, and are boiled with malted barley for several hours before fresh spruce shoots are added for a short time prior to fermentation. The ale takes its name from the ancient Gaelic name for Scotland, and is principally available during the summer months, both in cask and bottled formats.

EBULUM (6.5%)

Elderberry black ale, which takes its name from an ancient Welsh word for elderberry. Elderberry black ale was probably introduced to Scotland in

*the ninth century from Wales, and Williams's version is brewed to a
domestic Highland recipe from the sixteenth century. Elderberries were
used in a number of natural remedies, and were effective in alleviating
neuralgia, rheumatism and even influenza, due to the fruit oils and tannin
that they contain. Ebulum is brewed using roasted oats, wheat and barley
boiled with herbs and then fermented with ripe elderberries. Elderberries
fruit in Scotland during late September and into October, so Ebulum tends
to be available from October to January. It is a rich, very dark ale, with a
distinctive fruity aroma, a soft texture, roasted flavour, and a delicate
finish. Available in cask and bottled formats.*

FRAOCH HEATHER ALE (4.1%, bottled at 5.0%)

*Fraoch is tawny-coloured, and has a herbal, heathery aroma, with a
distinct whiff of peat. Full-bodied, malty and spicy, with a dry, apple-like
finish. The heather flowers are taken from wild, organic heather during a
short picking season of five to six weeks, so sufficient must be harvested to
ensure there is enough for a full year's brewing requirements. Flowering
ling and bell heather is used, and more than a million bottles are now sold
per year. Half of the heather content is boiled in a copper with hops and
ginger, while the remainder is placed in the hop back—where the wort is
collected after boiling. Recalling that the Picts used to drink heather ale to
give them courage before going into battle, Williams says of his Fraoch, 'It's
got everything in it that the Picts would have in their drink, but balanced
for a twenty-first-century palate.' Fraoch was a Bronze award winner in
the Speciality Beer category of the 2000 Great British Beer Festival.
A herbal, unhopped 5.4% version, called Pictish Ale, is produced during
December/January as part of the brewery's seasonal range.*

GROZET (5.0%)

*A gooseberry and wheat ale, with the addition of bog myrtle—a frequent
substitute for hops—for bittering purposes. The gooseberries are added
during the secondary fermentation, and give the ale its name. Grozet is*

derived from the Gaelic word for gooseberry—groseid. The ale dates back at least to the sixteenth century, and Tibbie Shiels—hostess at her eponymous inn in the Borders—was famed for her 'green grozet', which was praised, and consumed, by James Hogg (the 'Ettrick Shepherd'), Sir Walter Scott and Robert Burns. Grozet is pale gold in colour, with a fruity nose and a refreshing, clean, wheaty flavour.

Introduced to the range in 1996. Gooseberries fruit in Scotland during August, so Grozet tends to be available from September through the winter months, in both cask and bottled formats.

KELPIE (4.4%)

Organic seaweed ale, launched during 2000, and originally developed in association with the Clockwork Beer Co. in Glasgow, whose customers were soon drinking in excess of 100 pints per day, no doubt spurred on by the fact that seaweed contains natural constituents which will lower cholesterol levels and so is beneficial to the heart. Kelpie takes its name from the mythical Scottish sea horse, but there is also a pun on the word kelp, which is a kind of seaweed. Kelpie is an attempt to recreate the style of beer produced in coastal Scottish breweries before the middle of the nineteenth century. The barley was grown on fields fertilised with seaweed, which imparted its flavour to the finished ale. Fresh Argyllshire bladder wrack from Arisaig is mashed with organic malt to give Kelpie its distinctive maritime aroma and flavour. A rich, powerful, full-bodied dark ale, significantly malty from the dark roasted malts used, and with a slightly salty finish. The beer world's equivalent of a Campbeltown or even a light Islay single malt whisky! Available in cask and bottled formats.

PALEY ALEY (3.9%)

Well-hopped session draught pale ale, which takes its name from the fact that in the West of Scotland Pale Ale was commonly known as 'Paley Aley'.

HOUSTON

*Houston Brewing Company, South Street,
Houston, Renfrewshire PA6 7EN*
www.houston-brewing.co.uk

tel: 01505 612620 *fax*: 01505 614133 *email*: caroline@houston-brewing.co.uk

The Houston Brewing Company was established in 1997 in a converted, disused cellar of the popular Fox & Hounds pub and restaurant in the conservation village of Houston, just five minutes' drive from Glasgow Airport.

The Fox & Hounds is a listed building dating from 1780, when it was established as one of a string of coaching inns in Renfrewshire and Lanarkshire. A viewing window in the pub allows customers to observe the brewery in action.

The Wengel family has owned the Fox & Hounds for more than 20 years, and husband and wife Carl and Caroline Wengel decided to begin brewing their own beers after first introducing cask ale to the pub in the early 1990s. Brewing plant with the capability of producing 40 barrels per week was acquired from the Marston Moor Brewery near York, and an average of 30 barrels per week are currently brewed.

From its origins as a brew-pub, Houston has expanded to the point where it now directly supplies some 200 outlets across Scotland, and also sells into Cumbria. Cask Houston ales can be found further south in England due to the efforts of a number of distributors.

According to Caroline Wengel, however, 'We are happy to be small, and to be able to operate at a level where everything is hand-crafted. We have no real ambition to be any bigger. As it is, we can control the quality properly, and the head brewer oversees every brew.'

Peter's Well is available in bottled form from a range of selected outlets throughout Scotland. The Houston Brewery anticipates that the beer will become easier to find in shops during 2001. Peter's Well is actually brewed and bottled at the **Forth** Brewery in Alloa, but Caroline Wengel points out that unlike many 'contract' brewing arrangements, Houston's head brewer goes to Alloa each time a batch of Peter's Well is being produced, and oversees the brewing process, which takes place using Houston's own yeast.

In addition to the regular range of cask beers brewed by Houston, a number of 'house' ales are also produced for other outlets to sell under their own brand names.

Brewery tours—including a 'tasting tray'—are available by arrangement, and a range of polo and T-shirts, beer mats and posters may be purchased. Also available are the brewery's beers, in polypins (36-pint containers), 9- or 18-gallon casks, or for more modest occasions, in four-pint 'carry casks'. Peter's Well may be bought from the brewery in cases of a dozen bottles.

BAROCHAN (4.1%)
Celtic heritage and imagery feature prominently in the Houston brewing operation, and Barochan is named after a Celtic cross, formerly situated on a hillside near Houston, but now in Paisley Abbey for safe keeping. The beer is ruby in colour, and brewed using roasted barley, giving a lingering maltiness.

CHAMPION (4.0%)
One of the 'Four Seasons' range of seasonal ales, Champion is brewed during the summer months, and is a pale-gold beer, flavourful and hoppy.

FORMAKIN (4.3%)
A seasonal ale, brewed in the spring months, Formakin takes its name from the Formakin Estate, near Houston. Formakin is fruity and malty, with a hoppy flavour and a dry, malty aftertaste.

JOCK FROST (4.5%)
Brewed from December to February, Jock Frost is a full-bodied and well-balanced bitter, comparatively strong, and ideal for keeping out the cold.

KILLELLAN (3.7%)

Killellan is an ancient name for Houston, and this golden ale is mellow and refreshing, with a surprisingly lengthy finish.

PETER'S WELL (4.2%)

When the Celts were converted to Christianity during the fifth century, they named an ancient well with reputed healing powers, located near Houston, after St Peter. The beer has a rich, golden colour and a hoppy, fruity aroma and flavour. Quite light and refreshing in character. Bronze award-winner in the Best Bitter category of the 2000 Great British Beer Festival, and a runner-up in the 2000 Champion Beer of Scotland competition. Currently the only Houston product to be bottled. Originally called St Peter's Well, until objections from the St Peter's Brewery in Suffolk necessitated a change of name!

TEUCHTER (4.8%)

A seasonal ale brewed during the autumn months. 'Teuchter' is a Scots dialect word for a highlander, with the implication of lack of sophistication, but this beer is far from rough and ready, being a delicious, strong, dark, characterful Scottish ale.

TEXAS (4.5%)

The picturesque Renfrewshire village which is home to the brewery is a long way from its southern USA namesake in all senses, but this beer is brewed using American hops, hence the name. Texas is amber-coloured and full-bodied, with a very hoppy and fruity aroma.

INVERALMOND

The Inveralmond Brewery Ltd, 1 Inveralmond Way,
Perth PH1 3UQ
www.inveralmond-brewery.co.uk
tell/fax: 01738 449448 *email:* info@inveralmond-brewery

The Inveralmond Brewery was founded in Perth in 1997 by husband-and-wife team Fergus and Ailish Clark. Ailish is a native of Perth, while Fergus hails from Glasgow. Prior to starting up Inveralmond, Fergus spent ten years working for Ruddles in Rutland, Courage in London and, latterly, at the Tyne Brewery in Newcastle, having gained a BSc in Brewing and Microbiology at Heriot-Watt University in Edinburgh.

Fergus Clark is now assisted in the brewing by Ken Duncan, a Scot who gained considerable brewing experience in Australia before returning to his native land.

The opening of Inveralmond restored brewing to Perth for the first time since Wright & Co's North Methven Street brewery was bought by Vaux in the early 1960s, and subsequently closed. (See Heritage section.)

The Inveralmond Brewery is situated in a modern industrial estate on the northern outskirts of the city, and brewing takes place in a 10-barrel stainless-steel plant. Some 20 barrels are brewed each week, and around 150 outlets are supplied directly with casks. Several wholesalers additionally supply pubs throughout Britain.

Bottled Inveralmond ales are currently brewed and bottled under contract by the **Forth** Brewery in Alloa, but cask sales account for some 90% of the total Inveralmond output. The brewery numbers Canada among its export markets, and plans to expand its overseas sales in the future.

Bottled ales are available in branches of Safeway and Sainsbury supermarkets, along with the Oddbins off-licence chain, and a wide range of specialist outlets. Inveralmond products may also be purchased directly from the brewery, along with items of branded merchandise. Fergus Clark notes, 'We have an off-sales licence, and we'll sell anything from a single bottle to a nine-gallon cask with a hand pump for a party.'

In addition to its range below, the Inveralmond Brewery also produces a number of 'house' ales, including Friar's Tipple for Perth's Greyfriars pub, and Prince of Wales Ale for the Prince of Wales in Aberdeen. A limited edition 4.2% ale called Glamis Golden Pride was brewed in 2000 to mark the Queen Mother's 100th birthday. Inveralmond was the only Scottish brewery represented by invitation of CAMRA at the Queen Mother's Bar, which was a feature of the Great British Beer Festival at Olympia in London.

Inveralmond brews four seasonal ales, namely the spring beer Amber Bead (4.1%), which is amber-coloured and lightly flavoured with honey; the light, fruity summer ale Inkie Pinkie; (3.7%), the autumnal Pint Stowp porter (4.2%); and the malty, full-flavoured strong winter ale, Pundie.

The brewery is not really geared to visits by the public, but interested individuals will be shown around by staff if time permits.

INDEPENDENCE ALE (3.8%)
Inveralmond's first beer, Independence is a well-balanced, hoppy, fruity, draught session ale, with a suggestion of spice on the nose and palate. More full-bodied that might be expected for the strength.

LIA FAIL (4.7%)
Smooth, dark and full-bodied, with a distinctive malty flavour and an aroma of hops. Lia Fail is Gaelic for 'Stone of Destiny', the coronation stone for Scottish kings from 840AD until its removal to England by King Edward I in 1296. The stone was originally situated at Scone Palace, near Perth, and is now at Edinburgh Castle. Available in cask and bottled formats.

OSSIAN'S ALE (4.1%)
Pale-gold, full-bodied, fruity, yet quite bitter and hoppy.
Ossian was a legendary third-century warrior and bard, the son of Fingal, reputedly buried in the Sma' Glen near Perth. Ossian's Ale was launched in October 1997, and was a CAMRA Beer of the Year in 1999. Available in cask and bottled formats.

THRAPPLEDOUSER ALE (4.1%)
A refreshing, thirst-quenching, amber-coloured draught ale, with a strong aroma of hops. Thrapple is Scots for throat. Thrappledouser won an award as the Premium Bitter Ale at the 2000 Portsmouth and South-east Beer Festival, which came as a surprise to its brewers, who had no idea that it had even been distributed that far south!

IRIS ROSE

Iris Rose Brewery, Royal Hotel, High Street,
Kingussie, Inverness-shire PH21 1HX
tel: *01540 661898* **fax**: *01540 661061*

The Iris Rose began to brew in the summer of 1997 under the auspices of the late Bernard Justice, whose son Carl has now taken over the operation. Aged just 18, Carl must be the youngest brewery boss in Britain, and he started to learn the business of brewing from his father during weekends and holidays while still at school. The brewery takes its name from the fact that Carl's mother is called Rose and her mother was Iris.

The Iris Rose is located in converted outbuildings to the rear of the Royal Hotel, and is a two-and-a-half-barrel plant. In summer, two or three brews are undertaken each week, but in winter that drops to just one. Virtually all of the beer produced by the Iris Rose is sold in the two family-owned hotels, the Royal in Kingussie, and the Mains in nearby Newtonmore, though casks may be purchased on a 'buyer collects' basis.

The Kingussie Beer Festival has been established for a decade now, and takes place every November. In 2000 it featured some 60 beers, with Carl Justice brewing an 8.5% festival special to stand alongside his regular Iris Rose range.

The brewery has produced many specials, including Carl's Best Bitter, Ginger Ale, Harpole IPA, Liquorice Kingussie, Summer Ale and Zoe's Old Grumpy. Some of the most popular ones make reappearances from time to time, while new brews are regularly trialled. During 2000, Carl Justice brewed a very well-received red-coloured beer at 4.0% called Monarch of the Glen, which reflected the fact that the popular BBC television series of the same name was filmed in the Strathspey area not far from Kingussie. According to Carl, 'Monarch' may be back on the menu in 2001.

Brewery tours may be arranged.

BLACK FIVE (5.0%)
A dark ruby-coloured traditional Scottish ale. This beer takes its name from the type of steam locomotive that was added to trains on the Highland Line between Perth and Inverness in order to give them the power to climb over Drumochter and Slochd summits.

CRAIG BHEAG (4.3%)
A 'real ale' lager, brewed traditionally, and regularly available during the summer months.

GYNACK GLORY (4.4%)
A dark, sweet ale, but well-hopped and slightly bitter, too. The Gynack is a local river.

ROSEBURN BITTER (3.8%)
Typical English session bitter in style. Very drinkable.

STRATHSPEY HEAVY (4.6%)
Classic Scottish heavy beer, strong and characterful.

ISLE OF SKYE

Isle of Skye Brewing Company, The Pier, Uig,
Isle of Skye IV51 9XY
www.skyebrewery.co.uk

tel: 01470 542477 *fax*: 542488 *email*: info@skyebrewery.co.uk

The Isle of Skye Brewery, or Leann an Eilein in Gaelic (Ales from the Island), was established in purpose-built premises at the Skye ferry port of Uig in December 1995. Its ten-barrel brew-plant was assembled from a variety of sources, with some of the equipment being new and some reconditioned. The brewery's arrival gave Skye a second alcohol-producing facility to stand alongside the famous Talisker distillery. In fact, the brewery offices were located in the former excise officer's house at Talisker, before the whole operation was consolidated at Uig in December 2000. At the time of its creation, Leann An Eilein was the only brewery operating in the West Highlands and Islands area, though it has since been joined by the Isle of Arran Brewery.

The Isle of Skye was founded by Portree High School business studies teacher Angus MacRuary and his colleague Stephen Tinney, whose brainchild the project was, though Tinney's share of the business was purchased by MacRuary in 1997. The current Brewery Manager and Head Brewer is Eric Jones.

In 1998 the brewery opened its own bottling facility, and Angus MacRuary decided it was time to put away his chalk and concentrate solely on a 'proper' job, having previously combined teaching with brewing—though not at the same time.

'Like lots of professional micro-brewers, I started out as a keen home-brewer,' says Angus, who is something of a rarity in that he is a native of the area where he runs his Scottish brewery.

Demand for Isle of Skye beers in bottled format now outstrips the brewery's capacity, so the bulk of the bottled range is brewed and bottled under contract by **Belhaven**, who serve the supermarket and export markets, while Skye-bottled ales are sold on the island and in the West Highlands. The beers produced by Belhaven differ from their island counterparts by being branded Black Cuillin Dark Scottish Ale and Red Cuillin Scottish Export Ale. Bottled Isle of Skye beers are available in Safeway and Sainsbury supermarkets, the Scottish Co-op, and the Oddbins off-licence chain.

Around a dozen Skye hotels and bars now sell the brewery's cask beers, and a total of 70 Scottish outlets are served direct, while others further afield are supplied via wholesalers. Skye ales can be found in the deep south of England in cask format, though they tend to appear principally in winter, as the brewery works at full capacity during the summer supplying seasonal markets in the West Highlands and Islands.

The Isle of Skye Brewing Company has developed lucrative export markets in the USA, Canada and Japan, not to mention New Zealand and Iceland!

The existing brew plant can turn out up to 30 barrels per week, and bottling runs consist of some 1,500 bottles. By contrast, Belhaven's bottling runs tend to be closer to the 15,000 mark. During 2001, a new brewhouse and grain loft are being built at the Skye Brewery, which will increase its capacity to 25 barrels.

Brewery honours come in many forms, and the British Beermat Collectors Society voted the Red Cuillin mat British Beermat of the Year 1996, and two years later the society voted the brewery's set of four mats British Beermat Set of the Year 1998.

Isle of Skye brews a number of seasonal and occasional ales, including Extortion Ale (4.3%), which was produced in support of the campaign against tolls on the Skye Bridge!

Around a dozen 'house' ales are also produced, principally for outlets in the Highlands and Islands, though Coruisk Ale (4.5%) is brewed for the popular Britannia Inn at Elterwater in the heart of the English Lake District, and in 2000 the brewery produced Midge Ale (4.3%) for the historic Clachnaharry Inn on the outskirts of Inverness. According to David Irvine of the Clachnaharry, 'The ale is 4.3% in strength, so it does have a good bite to live up to its name.' Whether it will ward off the Highland pests is another matter, however, though Irvine says, 'I think a few pints could help you forget about the itching midge bites.'

The brewery shop is open from 9.00 am to 6.00 pm, Monday to Saturday, between April and October, and 12.30 pm to 4.00 pm on Sundays. Restricted hours operate during the winter months. It sells bottled Isle of Skye beers, along with a wide range of branded merchandise and other Scottish beers and general souvenirs. A number of the products on sale in the shop may also be purchased online. Brewery tours are available by arrangement.

BLACK CUILLIN (4.5%)

A full-bodied, smooth, dark ale. Rolled roast oatmeal gives it a distinctive, almost stout-like, bitterness, but this is tempered by the addition of heather honey. Black Cuillin is named after the principal mountain range of Skye on account of its dark colour. Available in cask and bottled formats.

BLAVEN (5.0%)

A powerful, full-bodied, malty golden ale. Fruity, refreshing and hoppy on the nose and palate. Blaven takes its name from Bla Bheinn, another Skye mountain, though this beer was originally named Avalanche when it was launched as a winter 'special'. Its popularity meant that it was added to the permanent range, and the name change reflected its move to all-year-round availability. An award-winning beer at the Overton Festival. Available in cask format, and first bottled during 1999.

HEBRIDEAN GOLD (4.3%)

An unusual ale, with a distinctive bitter flavour, which comes from the use of porridge oats. A smooth beer with a deep, creamy head. Originally only sold in bottles, but also available in cask since 1999 because of its popularity. A CAMRA Beer of the Year 2000 (Speciality Beers category).

RED CUILLIN (4.2%)

Malty, nutty, quite aromatic ale, reddish in colour, hence being named after the island's other, red-coloured, Cuillin mountains. Red Cuillin is the brewery's best-known product and has won a number of awards, including third place in the 1998 Champion Beer of Scotland competition, a silver medal in the same event the following year, and Beer of the Festival at the prestigious Norwich & Norfolk Beer Festival. Also a CAMRA Beer of the Year in 1999. Available in cask and bottled formats.

YOUNG PRETENDER (4.0%)

Golden in colour, dry and refreshing, fruity, quite hoppy, with a light aroma and a comparatively bitter finish. This cask beer takes its name from Charles Edward Stuart, 'The Young Pretender', better known as Bonnie Prince Charlie. It was from the Isle of Skye that Charles escaped to exile in France after the abortive 1745 rising, which had attempted to restore the Stuarts to the thrones of Scotland and England. Young Pretender was first brewed in 1996 to commemorate the 250th anniversary of the ending of the Jacobite rising. Judged 'Best Bitter' at the prestigious Norwich and Norfolk Beer Festival.

MacLACHLAN'S
BREW BAR

57 West Regent Street, Glasgow G2 2AE
www.maclachlansbrewbar.com

tel: 0141 3320595 fax: 0141 3323007 email: info@machlachlansbrewbar.com

MacLachlan's opened for business in 2000 and is co-owned by Jack Cumming and Ken Callen. Bruce Williams of 'Heather Ale' fame was brought in to lend his expertise and experience to setting up the brewing operation, and he remains 'brewing consultant'. MacLachlan's is the only brew-pub situated in central Glasgow, though a century ago beer was being brewed in more than 100 bars and inns within a stone's throw of Glasgow Cross.

The bar takes its name from the Glasgow brewing company G. & T. Maclachlan of Castle Brewery in Maryhill, and later also of Duddingston in Edinburgh. (See Heritage section.) The building in which the bar is situated was built by Maclachlan's and served as their main offices. The company name and castle logo remains in an original mosaic feature in the entrance lobby.

Maclachlan's boasts Pictish-themed décor, but its central feature is undoubtedly the four dramatically sited, mirrored conditioning and dispensing tanks, which stand on a steel platform directly above the bar. Each tank holds 1,440 pints, and between three and a half and five barrels of beer are brewed at a time.

In addition to the two beers regularly brewed on the premises, Maclachlan's offers a range of occasional and seasonal ales that has included honey beer, elderflower beer, strawberry beer and, late in 2000, a gooseberry and rowanberry wheat beer called Red Dalrigh. Cu Chullain is regularly available during the winter months, and the bar also stocks the full range of Heather Ale products in bottles. Fraoch itself is for sale on draught, in addition to two guest ales and an international selection of other draught and bottled beers and lagers. Maclachlan's also stocks an extensive range of old and rare bottlings of malt whiskies.

Brewery tours may be arranged.

MACLACHLAN'S CU CHULLAIN (6.5%)

Named after the legendary Celtic warrior, Cu Chullain is a distinctive beer made from porridge oats. Like all the MacLachlan brews, it features only GM-free, organic ingredients. Dark in colour, with a smooth texture and a thick, creamy head. Fruity, with a dry finish.

MACLACHLAN'S KÖLSCH (4.1%)

A pilsner-style lager made from GM-free organic barley and hops, but more fruity and less bitter than many pilsners. An ideal session drink, Kölsch, which is short for kölschbier—literally 'beer from Köln' (Cologne)— is brewed only at Maclachlan's and in Cologne.

MACLACHLAN'S PALE ALE (3.8%)

Lightly-malted and spicy, with an IPA's distinctive dry, hoppy finish.

MACLAY'S

Maclay Group plc, Thistle Brewery,
Alloa, Clackmannanshire FK10 1ED
www.maclay.com

tel*: 01259 723387* ***fax****: 01259 216511* ***email****: info@maclay.com*

The Clackmannanshire town of Alloa was once one of the great brewing centres of Britain, owing to a ready supply of barley for malting, coal for heating purposes, and excellent hard water from the nearby Ochil Hills, while the finished product could be shipped conveniently to London and other markets using the River Forth. (See Heritage section.)

Alloa once boasted eight working breweries and, until the late 1990s, Maclay's Thistle Brewery and **Carlsberg-Tetley**'s Alloa Brewery continued to be major employers and brewers of large quantities of ales and lager.

Now, however, both lie silent, though Alloa's beer-making heritage is being continued by the **Forth** Brewery, situated on the outskirts of the Forth Valley town.

Although brewing ceased on the site in August 1999—at which time it was producing some 14,000 barrels per year—the Thistle Brewery in the centre of Alloa remains the Maclay Group's head-quarters and distribution depot.

The old Victorian tower brewery would have required substantial capital investment in order to continue brewing efficiently, and for the Maclay Group there were attractions in allowing other companies to brew and bottle for them on a contract basis. Forth

Brewery now produces Coopers, Stirling and Thistle in keg format, and 80/- and Wallace as cask ales. **Belhaven** is responsible for the entire Maclay bottled range. Previously, bottling was undertaken by Frederick Robinson Ltd's Unicorn Brewery in Stockport.

The Thistle Brewery boasts a brew kettle dating from the building's construction in 1870, along with copper-lined fermenting vessels, and most of the plant remains *in situ* at the time of writing. It has been suggested that the Thistle would make an interesting Scottish brewing museum and visitor centre, fulfilling a similar function to the non-productive Dallas Dhu distillery on Speyside, but prospects for its survival do not look promising.

Maclay's began brewing in Alloa when local man James Maclay took over the lease of the Mill's Brewery in 1830, going on to build the Thistle four decades later on a nearby site adjacent to Younger's Candleriggs Brewery. When Maclay died in 1875, his two sons ran the company before selling it to the Fraser family of Dunfermline. The brewery was subsequently operated by the innovative Alexander Fraser, and by the time that Tennent Caledonian Breweries acquired a minority stake in the company in the mid-1960s, John Fraser Shepherd was chairman and joint managing director of Maclay's.

In 1991 Shepherd's widow, Helen, sold control to Evelyn Matthews and members of his family, who now own 85.1% of the shares. Since 1994 the holding company has traded as Maclay Group plc, with Maclay Inns Ltd and Maclay Wholesalers Ltd operating as subsidiaries.

Maclay Inns now has an estate of some 40 managed and tenanted houses in Central Scotland, while Maclay Wholesalers has more than 650 free-trade customers throughout Scotland. The Maclay Group employs in excess of 300 staff, and is one of the largest independently-owned family companies in the country's licensed trade sector.

In addition to the regular range listed below, the Maclay name appeared on six seasonal cask-conditioned ales during 2000. They included Tartan Scrum (4.5%), a brown ale produced in February, Tapsalteerie (4.2%), a Scottish cask lager that took its name from the Scots word for upside down, and was brewed in April, and James Maclay Anniversary Ale (4.8%), an ale based on an original 1830 recipe, produced in June.

The second half of the year saw the appearance of Hop, Skip & Drink (4.5%), a rich, mellow ale brewed in August to mark the Sydney Olympics, Hopscotch (4.2%), a strongly hoppy, intensely bitter October brew made using freshly-harvested hops, and finally Saint Nicholas (4.4%), a red-coloured, dry, spicy ale, brewed using crystal rye malt and mixed spices.

Also introduced in 2000/2001 is a range of seasonal bottled beers, primarily available through Safeway, with a small amount of distribution through selected on-trade outlets.

COOPERS (3.2%)

A comparatively recent addition to the Maclay range, along with fellow mixed-gas keg versions of the 60/-, 70/- and 80/- ales. Good session bitter for the non-real ale drinker.

80/- ALE (4.0%)

Russet-coloured, creamy, full-bodied and well-balanced. Quite hoppy, nutty and not too sweet, with a long, dry finish. Available in cask and bottled formats.

80/- THISTLE (4.0%)

Mixed-gas keg version of 80/- Ale, very smooth on the palate, with a tight, creamy head.

HONEY WEIZEN (5.0%)

Quite spicy and well-balanced top-fermented amber ale. Scottish heather honey and bog myrtle give it a distinctive bitter-sweet flavour. Available bottled.

KANE'S AMBER ALE (4.0%)

Cask amber ale with a hoppy aroma and a well-balanced flavour. It commemorates the late Dan Kane, a Scottish real ale aficionado and a key player in the successful move to restore Edinburgh's Caledonian Brewery to independence.

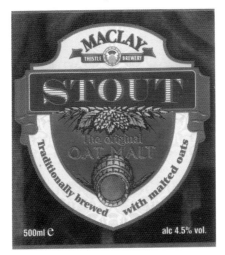

OAT MALT STOUT (4.5%)

Based on an 1895 recipe, the oats are malted, and pale malt, chocolate malt and roast barley are also included. This stout is densely black in colour, and has a decidedly smoky aroma. Malty-sweet, while the chocolate malt makes its presence felt in the finish. The malted oats make it a little more mellow on the palate than its better-known Irish rivals. Available seasonally in cask, and also bottled (as Maclay Stout). Maclay's label it as 'the only malt stout in the world'.

SCOTCH ALE (5.0%)

Strong, characterful Scotch Ale. Malty, full-bodied and appropriately sweet. Available seasonally in cask format, and bottled as Gold Scotch Ale.

70/- ALE (3.6%)

Copper-coloured cask ale, hoppy, with well-balanced aroma.

70/- SPECIAL (3.6%)

Smooth, mixed-gas keg version of 70/- Ale.

60/- ALE (3.4%)

Very drinkable, seasonal cask ale.

60/- STIRLING (3.4%)

Smooth, creamy, mixed-gas keg version of 60/- Ale.

THRAPPLE QUENCHER (5.2%)

Somewhat deceptive, in that its light body and colour suggest a comparatively weak beer. Thrapple (Scots for throat) Quencher has a hoppy aroma, refreshing and lemony, with a long finish. Available in bottled format.

WALLACE INDIA PALE ALE (4.5%)

Golden in colour, tangy and hoppy. Fruity, with a long, dry finish. Comparatively light in character. A nice example of the genre, first brewed during the 1890s. Available in bottled format.

HOGMANAY (4.0%)

A golden-coloured ale with a smooth, fruity taste and long, lingering finish.

TAM O'SHANTER (4.2%)

Tam O'Shanter is a full bodied ale with plenty of malty flavour and a rich, hoppy finish.

McCOWAN'S BREWHOUSE

Unit One, Fountainpark, Dundee Street, Edinburgh EH11 1AJ
***tel**: 0131 2288198 **fax**: 0131 2288201*

McCowan's Brewhouse is a flexible, modern micro-brewery, equipped to produce a wide range of products, from traditional cask and keg ales to modern lagers. The brewing equipment was imported from the USA. It adjoins McCowan's Bar in the modern Fountainpark development, within sight of **Scottish Courage**'s Fountain Brewery. The bar and brewhouse are owned by Scottish & Newcastle Retail, and opened in late 1999. A 'heritage area' is located above the bar, featuring a wide range of photographic and advertising memorabilia relating to William Younger & Co, along with a touch-screen TV system which explores the brewing process and the history of the Scottish Courage company.

The bar/brewhouse complex takes its name from William McCowan, the first chemist employed by Younger's (in 1877), and the man responsible for making significant progress in the development of brewing chemistry.

The creation of McCowan's means that Edinburgh now has four brewing facilities, and helps to redress the loss of the Rose Street Brewery and Firkin brew-pub outlets.

The Brewhouse is a five-barrel operation, and two brews are produced each week. The bulk of the beer is consumed on the premises, but casks are also sold to a number of managed houses in the S&N estate, and to independent outlets. Some have even found their way to Sweden!

Two regular Brewhouse beers are available on draught, and the resident brewer also produces many one-off and seasonal brews. It is anticipated that traditional Younger's beers will be brewed on an occasional basis, and the much lamented Younger's No.3 has already been produced as a 'special'. Other recent 'specials' have included Arctic Stout and a wheat beer, which was produced in 'bright' keg format.

Brewery tours on request.

80/- (4.5%)
Typical example of this Scottish beer style, sweet, with moderate bitterness. Roast barley is used in the mash, and the finished product is full-bodied, with a distinctive burnt caramel aroma.

IPA (3.7%)
Sweet, with distinct bitterness. Dry-hopped for a fruity aroma. Slightly resinous aftertaste.

MILLER'S THUMB

Miller's Thumb Brewing Company, The Canal,
300 Bearsden Road, Glasgow G13 1EP
www.millersthumb.com
***tel**: 0141 954 5333 **fax**: 9545533 **email**: canal@bigbeat.co.uk*

An American-style brew-restaurant, situated in the Glasgow suburb
of Anniesland, the Miller's Thumb Restaurant and Microbrewery
is housed in a restored and extended 1920s red-brick, art deco-
style, former timber-yard office building. The brewery opened on
4 July 1998, with brewing initially taking place under the control
of Indiana-born Jim Sanders, previously of Federal Jack's brew-pub
in Kennebunkport, Maine, USA. Sanders is now back in the States,
and current Head Brewer at Miller's Thumb is Colin Blackwood,
who trained in the USA, where he became a convert to the style of
ale being produced in microbreweries like Federal Jack's.

The Miller's Thumb micro-brewery is a seven-barrel operation,
and around 2,500 pints are consumed each week. The beers are
all American in style, carbonated and filtered, and six regular products
are on sale, though seasonal and special beers are also produced.
Most of the brewery's beer is drunk on the premises, though some
Independence Ale and Red Rooster is supplied to other outlets
in the ownership of leisure and entertainment group Big Beat,
who operate Miller's Thumb. The name apparently comes from
the fact that in days gone by millers often controlled the propor-
tions of pale and roasted malts used in beer-making. They would
give the 'thumbs up' sign when enough of a particular malt had
been added, or indicate by crooking their thumb that more was
required.

According to Big Beat, 'The microbrewery craze which is
sweeping America and the UK today has its roots and origins in
the great Scottish tradition of craft brewing, the time-honoured
skill practised by Master Brewers—beer experts who know how to

produce the freshest, most flavourful lagers and ales specifically to suit local tastes.'

The brewery shop is open during bar hours, and tours of the plant are available on request, Monday to Friday. Merchandise from jackets to bottle-openers is on sale both on the premises and online. Visitors may purchase a 'sample mat', which allows them to try six beers in one-third pint measures. Four-pint 'growlers' are also available to carry out a decent quantity of your favourite.

INDEPENDENCE ALE (4.8%)
Fruity and crisp wheat beer, with a rich grain taste and spicy hop flavours. Originally a seasonal summer ale, but now a 'regular', due to its great popularity.

LIGHTHOUSE ALE (3.2%)
Light-bodied, refreshing, low-calorie and low-alcohol beer, which still retains a distinctive flavour, with a malty aftertaste and floral aroma. Popular with reformed lager drinkers.

RED ROOSTER (4.1%)
Extremely malty Irish red ale in the style of Caffrey's. Full-bodied and smooth, lightly hopped and with caramel flavours.

MOLECATCHER'S (3.9%)
A well-balanced, malty, cream ale, smooth and easy to drink, with little or no hop flavour. The latest addition to the Miller's Thumb range, Molecatcher replaced the hoppy, porter-like Black Canyon, which may yet make a reappearance at some future date.

THUMB BLONDE (4.5%)
Golden export ale, smooth and drinkable. Citrus hop bouquet and malty sweetness. Colin Blackwood says that it reminds him of Stella Artois. Thumb Blonde is now available in bottled format as well as on draught, thanks to a bottling arrangement with Belhaven Brewery and a distribution deal with Scottish branches of Oddbins. It can also be found in a number of independent restaurants across Scotland.

WOODCUTTER'S IPA (5.3%)
Typical India Pale Ale, very dry, sharply fruity, assertive and hoppy.

MOULIN

RTR Catering Ltd, Moulin Hotel & Brewery, Kirkmichael Road,
Moulin, Pitlochry, Perthshire PH16 5EW
tel: *01796 472196* **fax**: *01796 474098*

The Moulin Brewery was established by hotelier Chris Tomlinson in the summer of 1995, when the Moulin Hotel was celebrating its 300th anniversary. The village of Moulin lies half a mile north-east of the popular holiday resort of Pitlochry, where a local brewery was in operation until the early years of the nineteenth century. 'Brewing our own beer was a way of enhancing the heritage of the hotel,' says Chris. 'It was a case of going back to the days when inns brewed ale for their own consumption.'

Between 1996 and 2000, James Mounsey's Aldchlappie Hotel at Kirkmichael, near Bridge of Cally, was a second Perthshire hostelry that made its own ale, but the producers of '1314' and '1707' beers have now closed down their operation, which was formerly the smallest commercial brewery in Britain.

The Moulin brewery is situated in buildings that were originally a coach house and stable block, and an initial five-barrel brew-plant produced around a dozen barrels per week. The capacity has subsequently been increased by the addition of extra fermentation tanks, though five barrels remains the average quantity brewed at any one time. 'We like to brew small and often', says Chris Tomlinson, who employs Alistair Dickson to do the actual brewing. The annual average output of Moulin is in the region of 500 barrels per year, though obviously, in an area with a substantial seasonal holiday trade, Dickson is kept busier during the summer months than he is in winter.

The 'make' is sold in the Moulin Hotel, and at the Tomlinsons' second hotel, the Atholl Arms, in the nearby village of Blair Atholl. It is also stocked in cask form by a number of other local outlets, and occasionally barrels find their way further afield.

Ale of Atholl has been available in bottle-conditioned format since July 1996, with bottling initially taking place on mobile apparatus, though a small Italian wine-bottling line was subsequently installed which can fill 300 bottles per hour. Since Easter 2001, bottle-conditioned Old Remedial has also been produced, and both bottled beers are available directly from the brewery/Moulin Hotel and from a number of specialist retail outlets, including Robertson's of Pitlochry.

Brewery tours are available from Thursday to Monday inclusive, 12.00 to 3.00 pm, and at other times by arrangement. The brewery includes a small retail area, selling bottled beers and branded merchandise, while serious sampling can be undertaken in the neighbouring Moulin Hotel.

ALE OF ATHOLL (4.5%)
The name is a pun on the Vale of Atholl, which lies close to the village of Moulin. A full-bodied, mellow, red-coloured ale.

BRAVEHEART (4.0%)
Well-balanced amber-coloured bitter, quite malty and sweet, named after the Mel Gibson film about the life of William Wallace.

LIGHT ALE (3.7%)
Refreshing, light-bodied, straw-coloured, hoppy session beer.

OLD REMEDIAL (5.2%)
Dark brown in colour, Old Remedial is a strong ale, brewed using roast malt for a characterful and assertive flavour.

ORKNEY

Orkney Brewery, Quoyloo, Stromness,
Orkney KW16 3LT
www.orkneybrewery.co.uk
tel: 01856 841802 *fax*: 01856 841754 *email*: beer@orkneybrewery.co.uk

The Orkney Brewery was founded in 1988 by English ex-civil engineer Roger White and his wife, Irene, in a former schoolhouse at Quoyloo, north of Stromness, on the 'mainland' of Orkney. White has been based on Orkney for some 20 years, and decided to re-store the island's long-dormant commercial brewing industry as a retirement project, little realising the scale to which it would grow. 'We started off brewing keg ales for the local market,' says Roger, 'and began producing cask ales as we developed markets further afield. Although most of our business now is in cask and bottled ales, we still produce a keg version of Dark Island for Orkney and Shetland.' Rob Hill, formerly of Moorhouses Brewery in Burnley, is employed as Head Brewer, and two other brewers are also on the payroll.

Peter Austin of the Ringwood Brewery in Hampshire set up the original Orkney brewing plant for Roger White, installing a ten-barrel facility, 'cobbled together from all corners of the globe', according to White, who recalls that pieces of equipment came from France and Wales, as well as England.

In 1995, a new brewhouse was built adjacent to the existing property in order to cope with increasing demand. There is now a capacity of 150 barrels per week, and the average annual output is in excess of 5,000 barrels.

A container-load of Orkney Brewery casks leaves the Orkney port of Stromness for the mainland on the St Ola ferry once a week, and via a number of wholesalers the beers find their way into pubs all over Britain, including a number on the south coast of England.

According to Roger White, 'Cask sales make up around 75-85% of our output, and the cask sales level is still rising, which is perhaps against the general trend.'

During 2000, export sales of bottled Orkney ales to the USA, in particular, grew dramatically, and Skullsplitter for the American market is contract-brewed and bottled by **Belhaven**. Quantities of other Orkney ales destined for bottled sales are tankered south to Dunbar, where bottling takes place.

Roger White and his team have experimented with bere (pronounced 'bare') ale, made from an ancient and primitive grain which is still grown on Orkney, but the yields from bere are so poor that production of bere ale is not commercially viable, particularly for a brewery that is already working close to capacity to satisfy markets for its existing range of products.

Tours are available by prior arrangement, and the brewery sells a range of pump clips, labels, bar towels, posters and T-shirts, which may be purchased by mail-order. There is an order form on the brewery website. Cask beers can be bought directly from the brewery. Bottles and cases of bottles are available from branches of Safeway, Summerfield, and Tesco supermarkets, along with a wide range of high street off-licences.

Dark Island (4.6%)

The Orkney Brewery's leading brand, and 'Champion Beer of Scotland' in 2000, having undergone a 'makeover' by brewmaster Rob Hill a few months before the championship took place in November. Hill altered the malt and hop content, the water chemistry, and even the sugar, in order to keep the brand ahead of a number of imitators, and the result is a beer described by CAMRA's Scottish Director Colin Valentine as 'a very malty, very Scottish beer. If beer was whisky, this would be it.' Dark Island was previously an award-winner at the 1995 Great British Beer Festival, and won a silver award in the Strong, Mild & Old Ales category of the 2001 CAMRA National Winter Ales Festival. As its name suggests, Dark Island is dark in colour, quite fruity, full-bodied and well-balanced. According to the brewers, it is ideal as an accompaniment to cheese dishes, steaks, and even hamburgers. Available in cask and bottled formats.

Dragonhead Stout (4.0%)

A strong, dark stout, in which the flavours of roast malt and hops predominate, and there is a powerful, dry, quite fruity finish. Described by its brewers as having 'the character and complexity of an Islay malt whisky'. Dragonhead won a silver medal at the Brewing Industry International Awards in 2000, and is recommended as an accompaniment to cheese and biscuits or a light meal. Available in cask and bottled formats, and named after the carved prows of the Viking ships that were once a familiar and frequently terrifying sight in the seas around the Orkney islands.

NORTHERN LIGHT (3.8%)

Pale-gold in colour, light and refreshing, nicely-balanced, with a fruity finish. The brewers recommend drinking it with fruit puddings! They also say that this is the beer to convert lager drinkers to traditional ale. Available in cask and bottled formats. Previously a seasonal special, but now part of the regular range due to its popularity.

RAVEN ALE (3.8%)

A golden-coloured, fruity beer, quite hoppy, with a bitter aftertaste. Its character is deceptive, as this could easily be mistaken for a much stronger beer. An ideal session drink. The raven was the emblem of Orkney's Viking earls. Available in cask and bottled formats.

RED MACGREGOR (4.0%, bottled at 5.0%)

The newest beer to join the Orkney list, Red Macgregor is smooth, malty and decidedly hoppy in aroma and flavour. The makers suggest drinking it with salads, pastas and light fish dishes, but also point out that it is a good 'session' beer. Available in cask and bottled formats .

SKULLSPLITTER (8.5%)

A strong reddish-coloured ale, named after the Seventh Earl of Orkney, Thorfin Hausakliuuf. This is a very smooth, fruity, drinkable beer. So drinkable in fact that the name can be dangerously apt if due caution is not exercised! A CAMRA Beer of the Year in 1999 and 2000 (Barley Wines category), and Supreme Champion Winter Beer of Britain in 2001—the first Scottish beer to win the winter gold medal. Skullsplitter is ideal, would you believe, with curries or chocolate. Available in cask and bottled formats, and Roger White says: 'We've been brewing it for about 12 years now, and it's amazing how much we sell in cask, considering it's an 8.5% ale.'

WHITE CHRISTMAS (5.0%)

As you would expect from the name, White Christmas is a seasonal brew, pale-brown in colour, with a nice balance of hops and malt, and a long, complex, fruity finish.

SCOTTISH COURAGE

Fountain Brewery, 159 Fountainbridge,
Edinburgh EH3 9YY
www.scottish-newcastle.com
***tel**: 0131 2299377 **fax**: 0131 2283584 **email**: info@scottish-courage.co.uk*

Scottish Courage is the largest brewing concern owned by a company based in Britain, and operates six UK breweries and one in the Republic of Ireland. It is responsible for some 30% of British beer production. Scottish Courage was founded in 1995, when Scottish and Newcastle plc acquired the Courage operation from Foster's. Scottish & Newcastle plc had its origins in a 1960 merger between Scottish Brewers Ltd and Newcastle Breweries Ltd, with the former company having been created by the amalgamation in 1930 of William Younger & Co and William McEwan & Co. (See Heritage section.)

In Scotland, Scottish Courage operates the Fountain Brewery in Edinburgh's Fountainbridge district. The total site covers some 22 acres, and the present brewery dates mainly from 1973, when it replaced the old McEwan's plant of 1856, which had itself been significantly upgraded during the 1950s. The 'new' brewery is situated on the opposite side of Dundee Street to its predecessor, though some of the old site is occupied by kegging facilities. Beer for kegging flows in a pipe over Dundee Street from the present brewery. The famous McEwan's clock, familiar to generations of Fountainbridge residents, was incorporated into the new Fountain Brewery.

Until 1986 Scottish & Newcastle also operated the former Younger's Holyrood Brewery, but its site has now been redeveloped, along with that of Younger's nearby Abbey Brewery. (See Heritage section.) When the Holyrood Brewery closed, some plant—including brewing vessels and kegging lines—was moved across the city to Fountainbridge. Latterly, Holyrood had specialised in producing Harp, Kestrel and McEwan's Lager.

The Fountain Brewery has a capacity of two million barrels per annum, and is equipped with one bottling line (capable of handling up to 36,000 bottles per hour), one canning line and two kegging lines. Early in 2001, however, it was announced that the bottling and canning facilities were to close during the next 18 months, with the loss of 170 jobs out of a total brewery workforce of 270. All non-keg packaging is to take place at the company's English breweries as part of a rationalisation programme. At the same time, it was revealed that a new £8m keg-packaging plant is to be installed at the Fountain Brewery, though that will not affect the level of staffing.

The brewery has a total capacity of 3m hectolitres per annum in terms of packaged output, though it currently operates around the 2m mark. All malt used is Scottish in origin, being sourced from Baird's Malt. Most of it comes from Inverness, though some is occasionally obtained from maltings at Pencaitland, south of Edinburgh.

Such is the global nature of brewing today that in addition to the McEwan and Younger brands traditionally associated with Edinburgh, Fountain Brewery produces Miller Pilsner under licence, and also Foster's Lager, though more Miller is produced than Foster's, as it is a significantly bigger seller in Scotland. McEwan's Lager is another major product, but sales of this have now been outstripped by sales of Miller.

Keg Younger's Scotch Bitter is brewed under contract in England, though it may be brought back in-house to Edinburgh in the future, while McEwan's Best Scotch Ale for canning is made at the Tyne Brewery in Newcastle.

The Fountain Brewery produces a range of own-label beers for a number of British supermarket chains, and a lager and an ale brand exclusively for export to Belgium are also brewed on the premises. The brewery now turns out approximately twice as much lager as ale, and between 70 and 80% of its output is for consumption in Scotland.

The Fountain Brewery once produced a range of fine cask ales, but the only cask product currently brewed there is McEwan's 80/-, which is tankered to the Tyne Brewery, where casking facilities for the Theakston range of cask-conditioned ales are located. Until the 1990s, the company produced Younger's Scotch Bitter, No.3 and IPA in cask format, along with McEwan's 70/- and 80/-.

Brewery tours may be arranged for groups.

KESTREL LAGER (3.0%)

*The Fountain Brewery produces some regular-strength Kestrel Lager,
though the bulk is now brewed at the Royal Brewery in Manchester. Kestrel
is a typical pilsner, with continental character and late floral notes.*

KESTREL SUPER LAGER (9.0%)

*Full-bodied, very strong lager, with distinctive continental character. A
good balance of bitterness to sweetness, and plenty of fruity, fragrant
alcohol flavours.*

McEWAN'S 80/- (4.2%)

*Smooth, medium-bodied Scottish ale. Sweet, with caramel and malty
flavours. Available in cask, keg and bottled formats.*

McEWAN'S EXPORT (4.5%)

*Medium-bodied export ale. Like many traditional Scottish ales, this beer is
sweet, with moderate bitterness. Light, fruity flavours can be detected,
though caramel, malty and burnt roast flavours predominate. Brewed in
Edinburgh since 1856, 'Export' is available on draught, in bottles and in
cans, and is the UK's biggest-selling premium canned ale. Not surprisingly,
it is the Fountain Brewery's largest ale brand.*

McEWAN'S LAGER (3.6%)

*Moderately full-flavoured lager, with a distinctive hop character which
gives the product citrus and floral notes. First brewed in 1976, McEwan's
Lager is one of the leading half-dozen standard lagers in the UK, and more
than 100,000 pints of it are sold in Britain every day.*

McEWAN'S 90/- (5.5%)

*Strong traditional ale, full-bodied, with a distinctive roast barley flavour.
Principally available in bottled form, and very occasionally as a cask ale.*

McEwan's No.1 (7.3%)

Award-winning, strong, dark ale, very malty and assertive, with hints of liquorice in the aftertaste. Only available in bottled form. The most characterful beer in the Scottish Courage portfolio.

McEwan's 70/- (3.7%)

Smooth, mid-gravity ale with a dry, fruity, spicy flavour which balances its sweet and roast characteristics. 70/- has traditionally enjoyed strong sales in Edinburgh and the East of Scotland.

McEwan's 60/- (3.2%)

An easy-drinking, dark-coloured Scottish ale. The flavours that pre-dominate are mainly roast and burnt characters. Principally produced for keg sales, though a proportion is canned.

McEwan's SPA (3.5%)

A new product for the Scottish market, SPA was launched in 2000. It was backed by an extensive promotional budget, and aimed at attracting lager drinkers and less committed ale drinkers. It is a pint with 'body and refreshment'. According to Scottish Courage, pre-launch research among the target 23-55 age group discovered that Scottish drinkers prefer 'a fizzier, more CO_2-led beer'. SPA is marketed as 'Scotland's Perfect Alternative', and its brewers say 'McEwan's SPA is best described as "fireworks on the tongue", with a CO_2 bite and a fruity citrus flavour combining to provide a great taste sensation.'

Younger's Tartan Bitter (3.7%)

Dark-coloured, comparatively sweet-tasting, medium-bodied bitter. Slightly fruity, with hints of roast barley. Available on draught and in cans. More Tartan Special is sold in keg format than in cans, and the largest markets are in the West of Scotland.

SULWATH

Sulwath Brewers Ltd, The Brewery, 209 King Street,
Castle Douglas DG7 1DT
www.sulwathbrewers.co.uk

*tel/fax: 01556 504525 **email**: info@sulwathbrewers.co.uk*

Sulwath Brewers Ltd was founded at the Gillfoot Brewery in Southerness, on the Solway coast, by Jim Henderson and local dairy farmer Bob Johnston during 1996, using converted farm buildings. Jim Henderson had been introduced to brewing at the now defunct Ledbury Brewing Co in Herefordshire, and he initially used recipes and names from the Ledbury range of ales, before beginning to customise them for his Galloway customers. He was born into a farming family in Peebles, and was a bank manager by profession before turning his hand to the more pleasurable business of making beer.

Prior to the creation of Sulwath Brewers Ltd, Galloway had lacked a working brewery since the Edinburgh firm of Campbell, Hope & King took over and closed the South Western Brewery in Newton Stewart in 1925.

Sulwath is an old name for the Solway estuary that divides England from Scotland in the west, and the Sulwath beers are named after famous local personalities and landmarks. The brewery logo consists of a depiction of the Galloway mountain Criffel, and two flying geese. The Solway coast is a great wintering ground for geese from the Arctic Circle.

Lack of space forced Sulwath Brewers to relocate during 2000 to the nearby town of Castle Douglas, where the family-owned company now trades from a converted bakery in King Street. A bottling room has been installed to cater for the three Sulwath products that are currently available in bottled format, and the new brewery has the capacity to keg as well as cask draught beers. Labelling and shrink-wrapping are also now undertaken in-house.

Anyone who claims that hops cannot be cultivated in Scotland should visit Jim Henderson's beer garden. He does, however, have an advantage over other would-be Scottish hop producers in that his wife's family are third generation hop growers in Herefordshire, where the Davis name is synonymous with the product. Jim's wife, Helen, is Sulwath's Marketing Director, while son Allen does the actual brewing and handles sales and distribution.

Sulwath is a member of Scotland's Craft Brewers Cooperative, along with **Bridge of Allan Brewery**, for whom Sulwath undertakes bottling.

Sulwath has a seven-and-a-half barrel capacity, and produces some 500 gallons of beer and lager per week, though in summer that figure may rise to 750 gallons and, at times, a night-shift is even employed in order to make sure production meets demand.

Cask ales are supplied to more than 50 outlets, while Criffel, Galloway Gold and Knockendoch are also available in bottled form from a range of off-licences. Criffel is stocked by Scottish branches of Safeway, who may expand their interest in the brewery's products in due course. Sulwath beers sell as far afield as the West Country and Shetland.

The latest introduction to the Sulwath range is The Black Galloway (4.4%), a very dark porter made using deeply roasted barley and chocolate malts. 'Robust, and an ideal winter warmer,' says Jim Henderson, who hopes to reintroduce the brew as a winter special in future years. The porter is named after the small, hardy, native breed of cattle that are found in the south-west of Scotland.

There is a smart visitor reception area that can accommodate up to 50 people, and a conducted tour of the brewery, along with product samples or non-alcoholic refreshments, costs £3.50 for adults, with children admitted free of charge. There is also a discount for group admissions. Beers may be purchased in single bottles or gift packs of three, though Jim Henderson will also happily sell you a case, a cask or a keg!

CRIFFEL ALE (4.6%)

A dark-amber ale, which takes its name from the most dominant mountain in the region. Complex, with well-rounded flavours of malt and hops, and a delicate bitterness.

CUIL HILL (3.6%)

A pale-amber, thirst-quenching light ale, with fresh malt and hop flavours. An ideal session beer, named after a ridge behind Criffel. 'Cuil' is derived from the Irish Gaelic for 'wooded hill'.

GALLOWAY GOLD (5.0%)
'Galloway's first native lager', according to its brewers. Brewed using lager and wheat malts and continental Saaz hops, Gold is refreshing, with a trace of citrus on the nose and palate. The lager was introduced in May 2000, and is usually supplied in cask or bottled format, but it can be kegged on request.

JOHN PAUL JONES (4.0%)
An occasional beer which takes its name from the founder of the American navy, who was born on a farm next to the site of the original Gillfoot Brewery at Southerness. John Paul Jones is described by its brewer as 'high in malt, with a nice malty taste and just a hint of bitterness'.

KNOCKENDOCH (5.0%)
Quite a dark, almost copper-coloured, full-bodied Scottish ale, brewed using deeply roasted malts. The ale has a pleasing hoppy aftertaste. Knockendoch gets its name from a prominent Galloway hill near Criffel.

TENNENT CALEDONIAN

Tennent Caledonian Breweries, Wellpark Brewery,
Duke Street, Glasgow G31
www.bass-brewers.com
***tel**: 0141 5526552 **fax**: 0141 5593398*

Tennent's is one of the most famous names in Scottish brewing, and the production of ale has taken place on the Wellpark site since 1556. (See Heritage section.)

From its modest beginnings as a family firm, Tennent's has grown to be a major brewer, and in 2000 it was acquired with its parent company, Bass Brewers Ltd, by the Belgian brewing giant Interbrew, in a deal that cost Interbrew £2.3bn. Interbrew is the second-largest brewer in the world, and had already gained control of another famous old British beer-making concern when it acquired Whitbread's brewing interests in May 2000.

Concern was expressed in certain quarters that Interbrew and Scottish & Newcastle Breweries would now have a duopoly in the British beer markets, with the former controlling more than 32%, and the latter 29%. As a result of a ruling by the Competition Commission early in 2001 Interbrew was ordered to sell off some or all of Bass Brewers.

Wellpark is the only surviving public brewery in Glasgow, though **Maclachlan's** Brew Bar and the **Clockwork** Beer Company have revived the old tradition of brewing on licensed premises in the city.

Tennent's was the first brewery in the UK to produce lager (1885), the first to offer lager on draught (1924), and the first to market it in cans (1935). Today, the company boasts that if you laid all the bottles and cans of Tennent's lager that are sold in a year end to end, the line would stretch to Perth—the Australian version, that is.

The famous red 'T' trademark was registered in 1876, and is probably Scotland's best-known brand symbol. In excess of £7m is spent annually marketing Tennent's Lager, and the brand has been the subject of many television commercials. Over the years such illustrious and diverse celebrities as Eric Morecambe and Bing Crosby have raised a glass of Tennent's to their lips in front of the cameras! Major sponsorships include the Scottish Cup and the T in the Park music festival.

The statistics of production at Wellpark Brewery are impressive. The equivalent of around 6,200 barrels of ale and lager is produced each day, and the high-speed canning line fills 2,000 cans per minute. There are more than 200 members of staff employed in production, yet thanks to a state-of-the-art computerised control room, one man per shift is able to run the entire brewery's production.

Wellpark has kegging and canning lines, but all Tennent's output destined for sale in bottled form is tankered to **Belhaven** Brewery in Dunbar, where bottling takes place.

Tours of the brewery and its excellent accompanying St Mungo's Heritage Centre are available from Monday to Thursday (contact Wellpark for details). The Victorian-style Molendinar Hospitality Suite is the starting point for visitors, but is also available for small-scale conferences and meetings, being equipped with comprehensive video and restaurant facilities.

SWEETHEART STOUT (2.0%)
Available in bottles and cans, this low-strength, sweet stout perpetuates the name of Younger's of Alloa, its original brewers, who were absorbed into what ultimately became Tennent Caledonian Breweries Ltd. It is said that the model for the now rather dated looking female figure on the Sweetheart label was the wife of one of the Everly Brothers singing duo. Not one of the company's best-sellers, but a survivor of a genre that is now dominated by two or three major industry players.

TENNENT'S EMBER 80/- (4.2%)
Mixed-gas delivery, premium session ale.

TENNENT'S LAGER (4.0%)
Scotland's favourite standard lager, with more malt and hop flavour than many of its competitors. Tennent's Lager sells in more than 30 countries, and some 625,000 pints are consumed on a daily basis. One in four of all

pints of beer drunk in Scotland is Tennent's Lager. It is the largest Scottish alcohol brand in any category, enjoying some 63% of the Scottish on-trade standard lager market in 1999. First brewed in 1885, and available on draught, bottled and in cans.

TENNENT'S LIGHT ALE (3.1%)
Easy-drinking, mixed-gas delivery. The market-leader for this style of ale in Scotland, where light ales still enjoy considerable popularity.

TENNENT'S SD (5.0%)
Full-strength premium lager, served on draught at 2°C, which is almost a third colder than most beers. When delivered, SD takes some 90 seconds to settle, giving a smooth body and a tight, creamy head.

TENNENT'S SPECIAL (3.5%)
Long established and popular with more seasoned beer drinkers, Special is delivered by CO_2 when on draught, and is a dominant beer in the Scottish off-trade market.

TENNENT'S SUPER (9.0%)
Well-regarded, malty-sweet yet slightly bitter 'super-lager', and one of the strongest brewed in Britain. Sales of Super account for approximately one-third of the 'super-strength' market, and 95% of sales are in the off-trade sector. The website www.superlager.com considers this to be 'first choice for any self-respecting drunk'!

TENNENT'S VELVET (3.5%)
Mixed-gas delivery. Easy to drink, quite full-flavoured, smooth ale, hence its name. Launched in 1995, Velvet has enjoyed year-on-year growth in both volume sales and market share, despite an overall declining market for ale in Scotland. Available in both draught and canned formats.

TENNENT'S WHITE THISTLE (3.1%)
Low-gravity keg beer. A smooth, light ale, based on an old pale ale recipe.

TOMINTOUL

Tomintoul Brewery Co Ltd, Mill of Auchriachan, Tomintoul,
Banffshire AB37 9EQ
www.tomintoul-brewery.com
tel: *01807 580333* **fax**: *01807 580358*

Founded in the heart of malt whisky country in November 1993 in an eighteenth-century granite and slate-built former watermill beside the Conglass Water, Tomintoul is Scotland's highest brewery. It was established by Kent-born ex-welder Andrew Neame, whose family are still involved in the old independent Faversham brewing company Shepherd Neame, though Andrew Neame subsequently left Tomintoul in 1996.

Tomintoul is equipped with a 20-barrel brew-plant, and has a weekly capacity of some 60 barrels. The Tomintoul Brewery Co Ltd went into liquidation early in 2000, and many of its assets were subsequently purchased by the **Aviemore** Brewery.

According to David Grant, Chairman of Aviemore Brewery, 'Tomintoul produces many fine beers, particularly Stag and Wildcat, and it would have been sad for those to have been lost. Our decision to rescue the brewery keeps the production in the Scottish Highlands.'

Some 80 Scottish trade outlets are served with cask ales, while wholesalers distribute both cask and bottled Tomintoul products outside of Scotland. Closer to home, Tomintoul bottled ales may be purchased direct from many specialist Scottish outlets, while wider availability is anticipated in the future.

Unlike the Aviemore Brewery, where some 80% of total output is sold in casks, Tomintoul retails approximately 50% of its 'make' in cask and 50% in bottles.

Tomintoul ales have become quite widely known, thanks to a degree of supermarket exposure, but this is not the first beer-making venture in Speyside to have attracted national attention.

Back in November 1897, the *National Guardian* reported the transportation of 350 hogsheads of Glenlivet ales from the Craigellachie Brewery by special train to Aberdeen, *en route* to a customer in the south. It took 18 railway wagons to carry the consignment, and the *National Guardian* noted of the brewery's Aberdonian agents, Gordon, Graham & Co, 'They must find the Glenlivet ale and stout—for there was stout in the big consignment as well as ale—much in favour with the public, otherwise they would not be able to get up orders in such volume as they seem to have the power of doing.'

The Craigellachie Brewery had been founded two years before the *National Guardian* report appeared, but despite the optimism conveyed by the newspaper coverage, the brewery did not thrive, due to difficult trading conditions and the fact that in Scotland's distilling heartland, beer had only very limited local appeal. The omens for Tomintoul a century later were not good, as Craigellachie ceased trading during the years prior to the First World War.

In the past, Tomintoul has produced a notably wide range of specials and seasonal ales, and it is the intention of the Aviemore Brewery to continue the policy of issuing some special and seasonal products, but less often than previously.

Culloden and Laird's Ale have been dropped from the regular range, which now comprises three ales, all of which are available in cask and bottled formats. For some years, Tomintoul bottled products have been contract-brewed and bottled, and the **Forth** Brewery currently performs those functions, though it is anticipated that all Tomintoul activities will be brought back in-house in the future.

It is hoped that during 2001 a dedicated visitor centre will be developed at Tomintoul Brewery.

NESSIE'S MONSTER MASH (4.4%)
Deep mahogany-coloured, fully-flavoured, malty ale with a fruity finish.

STAG (4.1%)
Dark in colour, malty on the nose and palate, slightly bitter.

WILD CAT (5.1%)
Deep amber in colour, Wild Cat is a strong, distinctive, smooth, nicely balanced mix of hop, malt and fruit flavours. It has quite an intense, fruity finish.

TRAQUAIR

Traquair House Brewery Ltd,
Innerleithen, Peebleshire EH44 6PW
www.traquair.co.uk

tel: *01896 830323* ***fax***: *830639* ***email***: *enquiries@traquair.co.uk*

Few breweries can enjoy a more palatial setting than Traquair House Brewery, which is situated alongside the Maxwell Stuart family's magnificent manor house near Innerleithen in the Scottish Borders.

Traquair House stands close to the River Tweed, and is reputed to be the oldest continuously inhabited home in Scotland, with some parts dating from the twelfth century. Traquair has been visited by 27 monarchs, and numbered Mary, Queen of Scots and Bonnie Prince Charlie among its house guests.

A brewery was in operation at the time of Mary, Queen of Scots' visit in 1566, and in 1739 a 200-gallon copper was installed in the brewhouse, located beneath the chapel.

The eighteenth-century brewery had been disused for more than 150 years when the 20th laird of Traquair, Peter Maxwell Stuart, rediscovered it in 1965, and set about restoring it to working order with the help of Belhaven brewer Sandy Hunter. Its demise dated from the time when commercial breweries were in the ascendant, and domestic brewing was becoming less common. Initially, when production resumed, ale was made to sell exclusively through the Traquair House gift shop, though demand soon began to outstrip supply.

Since the death of Peter Maxwell Stuart in 1990, the running of the Traquair estate and brewery has been in the capable hands of his daughter, Catherine, who extended the original brewery into an adjoining eighteenth-century stable block in 1993 so that capacity could be increased. The Head Brewer is Ian Cameron, who learned his trade from Catherine's father.

All the beer continues to be fermented in the original 200-year-old oak fermenting vessels, and a batch is brewed in the old premises every couple of months just to keep the equipment in working order. Brewing at Traquair remains a very traditional business and, as Catherine Maxwell Stuart observes, 'We've had trained brewers down from Heriot-Watt University in Edinburgh, but they tend to be a bit at sea when they visit because there are no buttons to press!'

Around 400 barrels are currently brewed each year, with more than 90% being sold in bottled form. Only a handful of outlets sell Traquair ales on draught, the most notable of these being the Traquair Arms in the village of Innerleithen. More than half of the Traquair output is sold overseas, principally Traquair House Ale and Jacobite Ale. The United States and Canada are particularly popular markets, along with Hong Kong, Japan and Italy. Bottling used to be undertaken by Belhaven, but bottling and labelling now take place at Robinson's Brewery in Stockport, with 50 barrels-worth at a time being tankered down to Cheshire every six weeks.

Catherine Maxwell Stuart notes, 'We didn't find any old recipes when we rediscovered the brewery, unfortunately, but we adapted recipes to produce a traditional Scotch ale style. The House Ale is similar to the type of 'wee heavies' you got in Scotland in the 1950s.'

Traquair ales in bottled format are available from more than 100 independent retailers in Britain, including selected branches of Waitrose. A range of beers and branded merchandise, including tankards, beer mats, posters, postcards and baseball caps may also be purchased directly from the brewery.

Occasional ales available on draught include Fair Ale, brewed annually for Traquair Fair in August, and Festival Ale. Limited edition bottled ales have included Wedding Ale, Silver Wedding, Catherine's 21st, Stuart Anniversary Brew, 100th Brew and 250th Brew, while Blair Ale was brewed in support of the Labour Party election campaign in 1997. The latest limited edition bottling is of 1,000th Brew, which, according to Ian Cameron 'was just one batch, brewed before Christmas 2000. It's a strong ale at 10%, and it should be available until the summer of 2001.'

The shop/brewery museum is open daily on a seasonal basis, and brewery tours are available seasonally by prior arrangement. Traquair hosts an annual Beer Festival each May, which acts as a showcase for Scottish brewers.

BEAR ALE (5.0%)

Bottled, since 1997, with limited availability on draught during the winter months. A hoppy, traditional Scottish 'heavy' ale, rich amber in colour, oaky and malty in flavour. It takes its name from Traquair's famous 'bear gates', which—legend has it—were locked when Bonnie Prince Charlie left the house, and could only to be reopened when a Stuart sat on the British throne once again. The gates remain locked.

JACOBITE ALE (8.0%)

Initially brewed in 1995 to mark the 250th anniversary of Bonnie Prince Charlie's abortive attempt to restore the House of Stuart to the British throne, but so popular that production has continued ever since. Remarkably characterful ale, with a hoppy, herbal aroma. Deliciously spicy, due to the inclusion of coriander, and with a suggestion of chocolate in the finish. World Champion Winter Ale, 1997, Gold Medal Beer at Stockholm Beer Festival, 1998. Occasionally available on draught, but principally bottled.

STUART ALE (4.5%)

A draught summer ale, launched at the 1999 Traquair Beer Festival. Stuart is a rich, amber ale, with a fresh, crisp, fruit flavour and subtle, bitter overtones. Bear Ale is now offered on draught from October to May, and Stuart replaces it during the summer months.

TRAQUAIR HOUSE ALE (7.2%)

Traquair's first commercial product, a strong, traditional ale, made using a little black malt blended with the pale malt. Beautiful russet tones, with hops, spices and chocolate predominating on the nose. Oaky and fruity on the palate, with vanilla and sherry flavours. A very long, fruity finish. Platinum Medal (World Champion Scotch Ale) at World Beer Competition, USA, 1997. Principally bottled, and available in a very limited number of outlets on draught.

VALHALLA

Valhalla Brewery, Shetland Refreshments Ltd, Baltasound,
Unst, Shetland ZE2 9DX
www.valhallabrewery.co.uk
tel/fax: *01957 711658* ***email:*** *sonnyandsylvia@valhallabrewery.co.uk*

The most northerly brewery in Britain, Valhalla is located on the northernmost of the Shetland Islands, and was founded in December 1997 by Shetland couple Sonny and Sylvia Priest.

Valhalla Brewery gets its name from the hall in the celestial regions, home of the Norse God Odin, where slain Viking warriors were taken after battle. There they were revived by a horn of ale, provided by a Viking maiden. The main doors of the brewery feature an artistic interpretation of a warrior's arrival in Valhalla. Shetland is, in many ways, more Scandinavian than it is Scottish, and the brewery name is very apt. Unst is actually closer to Bergen in Norway than it is to Aberdeen!

Valhalla is equipped with a four-and-a-half-barrel brew-plant, housed in a functional, modern building, and when demand is at its highest in summer, the Priests brew up to three times per week.

Given the brewery's remote location from the mainland—and even from Lerwick—it is not surprising that Sonny and Sylvia Priest concentrated initially on the market in the Northern Isles, but occasional barrels of the three regular Valhalla beers find their way south, sometimes as far as Wakefield, while the same beers are also available bottled in a number of specialist mainland outlets.

'Export' sales have been greatly aided by the installation during the summer of 1999 of a new, Czech-built bottling line, and a visitor centre and shop are planned for the future. In the meantime, a range of T-shirts, beer mats and pump labels are available from the brewery, along with bottles and casks of beer.

Brewery tours with complimentary drink (admission charge payable) are available by prior arrangement.

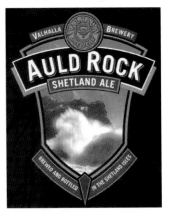

AULD ROCK (4.5%)

Valhalla's first beer, named after Shetland expatriates' affectionate name for their homeland. Dark and full-bodied, well-balanced hop and malt nose. A Scottish-style ale with a notably smooth finish.

SIMMER DIM (4.1%)

The newest product from Valhalla, Simmer Dim made its first appearance at the Shetland Folk Festival in April 2000, when it was provisionally named Festival 2000. The Simmer Dim is the brief period of twilight at midsummer in Shetland when the sun starts to rise again almost as soon as it has set. An attractive, light, golden, bitter beer.

WHITE WIFE (3.8% cask, 4.5% bottle)

White Wife takes its name from the ghostly apparition of an old woman, the White Wife of Watlee, who appears in cars driven by lone males on an isolated stretch of road not far from the brewery. White Wife is light in colour and body, a refreshing session beer. Bitter, with a fruity aftertaste.

Further Information

WEBSITES

www.camra.org.uk Principal site for the Campaign for Real Ale, featuring details of new products, beer festivals, general news and contact information for Scottish branches—including websites in some instances.

www.beerhunter.com Renowned whisky and beer writer Michael Jackson's dedicated beer site, with comprehensive information on beers and breweries of the world, tasting notes, and a useful search facility.

www.breworld.com Describes itself as 'the home of beer and brewing', and features material on the international beer scene, including publications, relevant organisations, events and beer-making. Also has a search facility and even a bulletin board for those who would rather type than drink.

www.protzonbeer.com Leading beer writer Roger Protz's website, with entertaining and informative articles on beers and bars, plus news and views, and a handy archive.

www.beersite.com Beer 'search engine' with more than 500 brewery site links, almost 300 'homepages', and even 200 home-brew related sites, though much of the material relates to the USA.

Bibliography

Anon, *A Short History of George Younger & Son Ltd, Alloa (1762-1925)* (Alloa, 1925)

Barnard, Alfred, *Noted Breweries of Great Britain & Ireland* (four vols.) (London, 1889-91)

Brown, George Mackay, *Winter Tales* (London, 1995)

Burns, Edward, *Scottish Brewery Trade Marks 1900 to 1976* (Glasgow, 1987)

Burns, Robert, *The Complete Works* (Edinburgh, 1867)

Carswell, Catherine & Donald, *The Scots Weekend* (London, 1935)

Dallas, John & McMaster, Charles, *The Beer Drinker's Companion* (Edinburgh, 1993)

Donnachie, Ian, *A History of the Scottish Brewing Industry* (Edinburgh, 1998)

Evans, Jeff, *Good Bottled Beer Guide* (St Albans, 1999)

Fairley, Jan, Gillon, Jack, McMaster, Charles & Moss, Michael, *Chambers Scottish Drink Book* (Edinburgh, 1990)

Jackson, Michael, *Great Beer Guide 2000* (London, 2000)

Jackson, Michael, *Pocket Beer Book* (London, 1997)

Keir, David, *The Younger Centuries* (Edinburgh, 1927)

Kenna, Rudolph & Sutherland, Ian, *The Bevvy: The Story of Glasgow and Drink* (Glasgow, 2000)

Lovett, Maurice, *Brewing and Breweries* (Princes Risborough, 1981)

Mackey, Ian, *25 Years of New British Breweries* (London, 1998)

McMaster, Charles, *Alloa Ales* (Glasgow, 1985)

MacNeill, F. Marian, *The Scots Cellar* (Moffat, 1992)

Protz, Roger & Sharples, Steve, *Country Ales & Breweries* (London, 1999)

Protz, Roger, *The Real Ale Drinker's Almanac* (London, various editions 1991-1997)

Protz, Roger, *The Taste of Beer* (London, 1998)

Ritchie, Berry, *Good Company: The Story of Scottish & Newcastle* (London, 1999)

Robert, W. H., *The Scottish Ale-Brewer*, (Edinburgh, 1837)

Titcombe, Graham & Andrews, Nicolas, *The Guest Beer Guide 1997* (Foulsham, 1997)

Townsend, Brian, *Scotch Missed* (Glasgow, 1997)

Various editors *Good Beer Guide* (St Albans, 1986-2001)

Various editors/contributors *Scottish Brewing Archive Newsletters* SBA, 1982-2000

Wright, Herbert Edwards *A Handy Book for Brewers* (London, 1907)

Yenne, Bill, *Beers of the World* (London, 1994)

Index of Beers

General Index